WHAT PART OF NO? DON'T YOU UNDERSTAND?

Avoiding and Defending Against

RAPE

By

Dennis G. Korby

ABOUT THE AUTHOR

Dennis G. Korby

Dennis Korby has a unique background that qualifies him to write this book. He is a black belt martial artist who has been practicing over 20 years, has worked in law enforcement and has counseled criminals as a lay minister. More importantly, and unfortunately for the bad guys, he is driven by an energy that causes others to describe him as "a man with a mission". Few people have more skill or knowledge. Virtually none has his concern.

C. Earl Todd, President,
Koto Press, Inc.

DEDICATION

This book is lovingly dedicated to Rita, April, Tim, Hannah, my mother Betty Korby, Brenda, Terry and to all women. It is also dedicated to the memory of my father Melvin Arthur Korby.

AUTHOR'S THANKS

I want to thank all the women who have shared with me their ordeals from the past, especially Madelyn and my sister Brenda.

I want to thank all of those generous people who read early drafts of the book and gave me their constructive criticisms and comments.

I want to thank Dan & Kathy Fisher, Janine Smith, Heather Smith, and Cathy Yount for their willingness to demonstrate the various techniques before the camera.

I want to thank Earl Todd, a black belt martial artist as well as the Editor & Publisher of this book, for his self-defense expertise, even more for his production & graphics skills, but most for his willingness to work untold hours to overcome all obstacles to expedite the book.

My special thanks go to my martial arts sensei, Tom Smith and his wife, Janine, for their enthusiastic technical support, advice and encouragement, without which I may never have finished.

Most of all, I want to thank my wonderful wife Rita and my children April, Tim & Hannah for their unending patience and understanding.

FOREWORD

Women have always been known as the weaker sex in physical confrontations and are often at the mercy of men purely because of their size and lack of force. Well, it's about time that women got smart and changed tables. Finally we have a book that will help us do just that.

Being a mother of four, and a public school teacher, I clearly realize the importance of this book. "What Part of No" shows women just how vulnerable they are and educates them from A to Z concerning this evil crime. This book forces the reader to analyze what she would do in different predicaments and offers several creative options for defense.

As martial artists, my husband and I have known the author for nine years and have actually participated with him in conducting rape prevention seminars. I can personally attest to his sincerity and dedication in trying to enlighten women on how to prevent a would-be attack.

I want to thank Dennis for all his time and effort it took for him to write this book. Dennis is right: "it's time to do our homework."

Janine Smith, Westland, MI
April, 1994

TABLE OF CONTENTS

TABLE OF CONTENTS

INTRODUCTION

Throughout this book I will reveal information, share my experiences and demonstrate self-defense techniques. I fully believe they can significantly increase your ability to avoid, and if necessary, defend against a rapist's attack. It is my contention that:

1. You **are not** as safe from being raped in this country as you might think or have been led to believe.

2. You **are not** as psychologically and physically prepared to defend yourself as you ought to be.

3. You **need** to read this book with an open mind.

4. You **must** be properly motivated and prepared to look the current rape epidemic squarely in the eye.

5. You **can** develop an effective self-defense system which includes principles and techniques designed to distract, confuse and deter a rapist.

I will try to convince you of the first two points, hope you adopt the mind-set of the third and prepare you for the fourth. The fifth point is entirely up to you.

At times, you might suspect as you read that I am trying to put you on the spot. Well, in fact, I am. You might find yourself asking whether I know what I am talking about. In fact, I do. You might also ask yourself, "Does this guy have all of the answers?" In fact, I don't. However, with the alarming number of American women raped each year, it doesn't appear that anyone else does either. No one bats a thousand. I simply want my turn at bat in attempting to help you in the area of rape prevention.

If the current rape epidemic (documented in chapter four) continues, and it probably will, a surprise test could indeed come your way as an attempted rape. If this ever happens, a rapist, whether acquaintance or stranger, will suddenly, unexpectedly and thoroughly test your ability to defend against him. How well you have prepared to defend yourself will become immediately evident. It is therefore imperative that you make preparation, not for the inevitable, but for the probable. You must do some rape prevention homework. I can help you do that. I have experience and academic training as a reserve police officer, have ministered as a prison/jail chaplain (layman). I have practiced and taught martial arts and have lectured to hundreds of women attending rape prevention seminars conducted since 1985. This background has given me an unusual perspective on the subject. I can help you with your homework, since I have a good idea of what will be on the test.

In the ministry and from lessons in life, I have learned that people are more alike than they are different. The old saying that "Boys will be boys, and girls will be girls," is generally true. The problem is that some "boys" for one reason or another, decide to rape what our society seems to suggest is the "weaker sex." Some socially commissioned "protectors" of women become their predators. Women, young and old, are then forced on a daily basis to distinguish the good ol' boys from the bad. It is not an easy task.

In researching and preparing for this book, I noticed that a prevailing attitude is shared by most women. Everyone seems to agree that there is an enormous rape problem in this country. However, like a terminal disease, its existence is acknowledged, but it ranks low on the list of things to think about. Mental processes such as "positive thinking," repression, and denial are used as a smoke screen to cover its lurking presence. Religious beliefs offer consolatory relief. But the problem with rape just does not go away.

The media, in all of its forms, offers daily reminders of its presence. You would have to be a blind cat in a dark room not to see it. The prevailing attitude repeatedly rises to the occasion. "I know it (rape) is out there, I just hope it never happens to me." "I know that children are being raped, I just hope that it never happens to mine." "I hope . . . "

"You can never run away from a problem. You must either face it or perish. If that be so, then let it be here and now."
- Robert Louis Stevenson

Let me suggest another line of thought - an attitude which looks this problem of rape squarely in the eye. I have always considered myself a realist who prefers optimism to pessimism. When it comes to women and rape, I truly believe that a realistic approach will benefit you most.

Life doesn't always meet you halfway. You never know when your car will stall. Perhaps late at night on a deserted highway, the engine will stop. You might find yourself exiting a store one night and for some unexplainable reason, the parking lot lights are off. The one time that you forget to lock your doorwall may be the night that some deranged rapist is creeping through backyards. Life is filled with uncertainties which you must take a day at a time. Life's surprises will come your way and they will go. A rapist may someday do the same. His presence will surprise you. Just make sure that you have a few surprises of your own. This book contains information which will help you do that.

It is time for you to learn how to outwit and outsmart a would-be rapist. Begin learning now how to psychologically, verbally and physically defend against rape. It is time to learn how to effectively ask a would-be rapist, "What part of NO don't you understand?"

Chapter One - WHAT WOULD YOU DO IF . . . ?

Nothing rivals a collection of the right questions to get to the heart of a matter. Any doctor, teacher, police officer, sales person, psychologist, parent or automotive mechanic will give a thumbs up to that statement. In conducting rape prevention seminars since 1985, I have often used a series of questions as a starting point. The questions were designed to test each participant's level of awareness concerning rape prevention. I asked what they thought they might do in hypothetical situations. Following are similar questions that were developed especially for this book. The questions are grouped into four categories. Category one involves questions to test your general awareness of the crime of rape. The following categories focus on situations involving confined areas, parking lots and traveling. My recommendation is that you answer each question on a separate sheet of paper. After reading this book, answer these same questions again. Compare your second answers to your first.

GENERAL AWARENESS

1. What is your definition of rape? What actions would make up rape in your mind?

2. What do you think is the legal definition of rape in most states?

3. How many rapes were re- ported (documented) in 1990?

4. Our Federal Government an- nually estimates the number of rape victims. Take a guess at what that number was for 1990?

What do you think the annual estimate was between 1973 and 1987?

5. What percentage of rapes are reported to police departments?

6. Why do you think women are reluctant to report being raped?

7. In 1990 how well did the United States protect its women from rape as compared to other nations?

8. Where do most rapes gener- ally occur?

9. When do most rapes occur?

10. Between what ages are most women raped?

11. How old do you think the av- erage rapist is?

12. What race of women is more likely to be raped than others?

13. Are most offenders armed with a weapon when committing rape?

14. What is the likelihood of a woman being raped if she physi- cally resists with self-protective measures?

15. What is the likelihood of a woman being injured if physi- cally resisting?

16. What is the average length of a rapist's sentence and what part of it is usually served in prison or jail?

17. Rapists typically have several advantages over their victims. Can you name five? Which one is most advantageous?

18. Can you name three things which offenders usually fear when committing rape?

19. When do you think you are most vulnerable to a rapist's attack?

20. Name five body parts where a rapist is particularly vulnerable. What would be your primary target?

CONFINED AREA

21. You are alone in your home, motel, dormitory, etc. and suddenly confronted by an intruder you have never met. Surprised and frightened, a terrifying thought occurs to you. Let's assume for this book that your intuition tells you that you are standing across the room from a rapist. There is no immediate means of escape. Without hesitation, he begins to lunge toward you. You have approximately one full second to respond. What would you do?

22. Let's assume that you are in an identical predicament as mentioned above. This time though the intruder is slowly walking toward you while trying to make some off-the-wall conversation. Again, you intuitively sense that the intruder has raping you on his mind. What would you do?

23. You are alone in your home, a motel, the dormitory, etc. with a man who is an acquaintance. What started as a friendly and "normal" conversation, is beginning to change. To your surprise, your acquaintance is suddenly using sexually suggestive language. He is attempting to get close to you. Embarrassed and frightened, you begin to back away. What would you say to him?

24. Concerning the above situation, what would you do if your verbal response failed to discourage his advances? Your "no" is not enough.

25. You are alone, lying on your back with a rapist sitting on top of you. Each of his hands is holding one of yours. His size and strength completely overpower you. It is abundantly clear to you that a disaster is only a few moments away. Feeling desperately helpless, you need to do something. What would you do?

26. You have just opened your front door. As you begin to enter, someone grabs you from behind and is attempting to push you inside. He is holding you with one hand and covering your mouth with the other. He orders you to go inside. Would you cooperate? If not, what would you do?

27. You are alone and in bed sleeping. You hear breaking glass, a door being pushed in, a door lock being jimmied. This alerts you to the fact that someone is trying to enter your dwelling. What would you do?

28. Gang rape, in which a victim is abused by several assailants, is perceived by most women as the most horrifying and traumatic experience imaginable. Many have described it as the ultimate nightmare. If you were in a confined area with several men and sensed that the chances of being gang raped were increasing, what would you do to calm the tide? If the men started fondling and forcing themselves upon you, what would you do then?

PARKING LOTS

29. What do you typically do to safeguard against abduction or rape when exiting a building or your home and approaching your vehicle?

30. As you are opening the door of your vehicle, you notice that someone is lunging at you. The assailant is approximately six feet away. You have less than one second in which to attempt some kind of defense. What would it be?

31. How would you respond to the above situation if the assailant were simply walking toward you and attempting to make conversation?

32. You are entering your vehicle in a crowded parking lot. A man suddenly enters the passenger side door, grabs you and orders you to back the car up and drive in a certain direction. He places a weapon against your side with a stern warning that any resistance will be dealt with immediately. He expects you to cooperate. Would you? If not, what would you do?

33. You are carrying a purse and a shopping bag. As you approach your vehicle, a van pulls up next to you. A man quickly exits and reaches toward you in what appears to be an abduction attempt. What would you do?

34. While walking, jogging or bicycling, someone grabs you from behind with a bear-hug. They are attempting to drag you behind some bushes or into a vehicle which suddenly pulls up. You need to do something to prevent the abduction and probable rape. What would you do?

TRAVELING

35. As you are entering a motel lobby, you are reminded of the predicament awaiting you. You are traveling alone and will be locking yourself into a room in a few minutes. Unfortunately, every time this happens, there is usually some anxiety involved. You are never quite sure whether someone is lurking behind the shower curtain or is under the bed. You are either locking an intruder out or locking one in with you. What could you do to alleviate these anxious moments?

36. You are alone and waiting for an elevator to stop at your floor. A man walks up behind you. The elevator door opens and the man politely motions for you to enter before him. No one else is in the area. You are uncomfortable with his suggestion, but waiting alone for another elevator doesn't appeal to you either. As you begin to enter the elevator, you need to decide where to stand? What would you do?

37. While driving alone at night on an expressway, your car stalls. You are forced to make an emergency stop. What would you do to safeguard against an attack and to summon assistance?

38. You are driving down a highway with a median dividing two lanes on each side. You are maintaining an average speed of about 45 miles per hour and are in the outside lane. You notice that a car which has been following you closely, pulls alongside. The two male occupants are taunting you and motioning for you to pull over. What would you do?

39. You are driving home and notice that someone might be following you. Since you have a few more miles before reaching your destination, you decide to verify whether your suspicion is correct. What would you do?

40. Unfortunately, when traveling on expressways after dark, you sometimes need to use a restroom. The women's rooms in rest stop areas are usually a lonely place to be at night. Gas station restrooms are generally located around the side of a building. What precautionary steps can you take to safeguard yourself?

Well, how did you do? Concerning the questions on confined areas, parking lots and traveling, are you certain that your answers would pass the test in a real life situation? Would a rapist describe your defensive capabilities as his worse nightmare or would he find them predictably weak and nonthreatening? These questions will be examined in chapters four and eight.

In the next two chapters, you will be introduced to two women who were forced to defend themselves against rapists. Unlike you, they did not have the luxury of sitting back and thinking about what they would do in hypothetical situations. All preparation time had expired. As you will see, their attacks demanded more, psychologically and physically, than they could give.

In Chapter Two an incident involving my sister illustrates how uncontrolled fear (panic) can totally incapacitate a woman in her attempt to defend herself. My sister's situation involved an attempted abduction. In Chapter Three, an interview with a woman who was raped by an acquaintance illustrates this incapacitating condition as well. Both women were unprepared to deal with the situation and both women panicked. In both cases, once the women panicked, the assailants had all of the odds in their favor. Let's look at each of their experiences.

Chapter Two - INTENSE FEAR

Fear is the father of courage and the mother of safety.
- Henry H. Tweedy

While conducting rape prevention seminars, I often ask participants to list for me the many advantages rapists generally have over their victims. Common answers include the rapist's strength and size, the element of surprise, the use of weapons, a planned (and usually practiced) attack, and the presence of more than one attacker. After a brief discussion of each answer, I usually focus on the rapist's number one advantage. It is a person's tendency to panic when attacked. This sudden onslaught of fear does more to incapacitate a woman's ability to defend herself than any other single factor. Since her fear is usually far beyond what she is equipped to handle, all systems seem to break down into a full blown state of chaos. According to Susan Brownmiller, just the fear of being raped in daily life is a heavy burden for women to carry. Brownmiller comments on how rape "has played a critical function" throughout history. "It is nothing more or less than a conscious process of intimidation by which all men keep all women in a state of fear" (Brownmiller, 1975, p. 15). Except for the generalization, her statement contains some truth.

John J. Poklemba, serving as Director of Criminal Justice in New York was quoted by the New York Times on June 19, 1989, "Few crimes are more universally condemned or fear-provoking' than rape." "Fear-provoking" is an accurate description when you consider what a woman risks during a confrontation with a rapist:

- Embarrassing exposure of her body

- Sexual violation

- Bodily injury

- Pregnancy

- Disease

- Loss or changes in existing personal relationships

- Death

According to Chezia Carraway, of the New York City Task Force Against Sexual Assault, "During a rape, a woman's life is out of her control," (Goodhousekeeping, 1989). In the same article, Meloney Sallie, community education director for Women Organized Against Rape in Philadelphia, recommends a physical exam soon after a rape "since shock will often make a woman unaware of any injuries." This shock condition insulates victims from the extreme pain and trauma. Women recovering from a rapist's attack are often surprised at the number of bruises and injuries sustained during the ordeal. In his book, Aftershock, Dr. Andrew Slaby examines the effects of trauma, crisis and loss.

Chapter Two - INTENSE FEAR

"There is nothing more frustrating than watching others decide your fate" (Slaby, 1989, p. 19). I will take the liberty to add to Dr. Slaby's statement, "There is nothing more frustrating" and frightening "than watching others decide your fate." Even the courts have looked closely at the extent of fear experienced by a woman during an attempted rape. Susan Estrich takes a well documented and researched look at how the "legal system victimizes women who say no." In one case she analyzes (State v. Rusk), the extent of a woman's fear significantly influenced the outcome of a rape trial. "Reasonably grounded fear" was required "to obviate the need for either proof of actual force on the part of the assailant or physical resistance on the part of the victim" (Estrich, 1987, pp. 64-65). Translation: The victim's fear of rape "had to be generated by something of substance." Simply being scared was not enough evidence to show forcible rape.

No wonder women often describe a "numbness" in their body and immediate disbelief during an attack. In a moment of time, the unbearable reality of the situation utterly destroys everything it touches. A woman's view of self and the world around her is suddenly and brutally shattered. This "numbing" is explained in The Rape Victim (Koss, Harvey, 1987, p. 26). "Numbing . . . represents the individual's attempts to slow down cognitive processing and reduce the anxiety associated with intrusive representations." In other words, the mind blocks out whatever trauma the individual cannot effectively handle. Sometimes the thoughts and fears associated with the trauma lie buried for months and even years. This condition, known as Post Traumatic Stress Disorder (PTSD) has been officially labeled as an anxiety disorder (American Psychiatric Association, 1980). According to Dr. Slaby, the causes for a PTSD "include extreme repression of the painful event, with defense mechanisms so efficient that they have helped put the trauma out of the victim's mind" (Slaby, 1989, p. 48). I believe that similar to the many veterans who experience this condition from the hazards of war, many women relive past sexual attacks.

The night my father was rushed to a hospital, I experienced firsthand how the mind and body sometimes deal with trauma and intense fear. On a Saturday night, I sat at a kitchen table studying for an exam. A phone call from a hospital informed me that my father had suffered a heart attack. No details were given over the phone. I feared the worse and hoped for the best. I took my Bible with me. The sight of it probably encouraged the front desk staff to allow me to enter the emergency operating section. God knows, I was not up to what I saw. I quickly glanced into a few empty rooms. In one of them, I saw my own father lying on a table with a medical team working on him. There he lay with his mouth open and blood all over his chest. Blood was everywhere. It was more trauma that I could handle. The sight of that would have destroyed my mother; it almost destroyed me. I felt numb, both physically and emotionally. Shocked senseless with fear, I tried to find refuge in disbelief. Each agonizing minute that passed reminded of how "fear hath torment" (I John 4:18).

After ten minutes had passed, I was then told that my father "was not going to make it." I remember thinking, "What do you mean he's not going to make it. He must make it, that's my father lying there." Although traumatized, I had to walk out in the waiting room and break the news to my mother. She was sitting on the floor just outside the operating room. That was as close to my father as the hospital would allow. She had her arms crossed and was rocking back and forth. As I turned toward her, she looked up at me with tear-filled eyes and said "Dad's going to make it isn't he?" I was fear-stricken, afraid that my dad would die and afraid to tell my mother. I looked at her and said, "It doesn't look very good, but I don't know Mom, God knows." My father died.

Whether it is a fear of being raped or as in my case, a fear of my father's death, the impact is much the same. Coping mechanisms are required to endure. In his book, Panic Disorder - The Great Pretender, Dr. H. Michael Zal offers a quotation from the New Harvard Guide to Psychiatry. Fear "involves recognition and arousal, with preparation for action. Both fear and anxiety are signals warning of impending danger which enables the person to take measures to deal with a threat," (Zal, 1990). This is commonly called the fight or flight dilemma. When it comes to rape however, I have noticed something quite peculiar. Victims often sense and feel the "recognition" and "arousal." They clearly heed the "warning signals." The difficulty is deciding what "measures" and "actions" should be taken. Herein lies the dilemma. The adrenaline is pumping while the mind is asking "What do I do now?" The present threat of a rapist will incite fear. Not knowing what to do amplifies that fear. To compound the problem, rapes are often committed at a time when women least expect it.

In later chapters, you will be advised on how to internalize techniques and principles through which the sudden fear of being raped can be channeled. You will also learn how to meet a rapist's element of surprise with a few surprises of your own. Interviews which I have conducted with rape victims, and those of others which I have read, repeatedly show that one or more of the following conditions are manifested during an attack:

1. Legs tend to weaken.

2. Thinking becomes confused.

3. Time seems to become distorted.

4. Breathing becomes laborious and difficult to control.

5. A sensation of tunnel vision intensifies the presence of the rapist.

6. Reality becomes difficult to determine in that the victim feels as if she is suddenly experiencing the attack both as a spectator and recipient. The experience is often described as a "living nightmare." The "it could never happen to me" illusion is instantly shattered. All sense of personal security is destroyed.

The following incident graphically illustrates how uncontrolled fear can overwhelm a victim and drastically reduce the chances of defending against a rapist.

On September 11, 1989, at approximately 8:45 P.M., my sister had finished her shopping a large and popular shopping center in Troy, Michigan. It was dusk, and according to my sister, "not dark at all." She exited the mall through a major department store. Like many women, she began her parking lot routine to safeguard against any

type of danger. Her standard routine consisted of:

- Having her car key in hand
- Exiting the store with others
- Quickly glancing around the general vicinity
- Walking "confidently" and attentively toward her locked car door
- Looking in the back seat, sometimes looking under the car
- Entering the car quickly and immediately locking the power door locks

Sound familiar? It should. My sister's routine includes the same things that most women do to feel safe and protected in parking lots. Why would she do anything else? Most police departments, schools, colleges, television programs, self-defense books and rape clinics teach and endorse these precautionary measures. The routine is indeed helpful and those who recommend it are certainly sincere. However, I want you to understand something. It does not offer enough protection. Why, you might ask? Every part of the routine is completely predictable. My sister's parking lot routine consisted of procedures which are common knowledge both among women and rapists. Any rapist lurking in a parking lot is expecting you to go through these or similar motions. Likely, he will have planned to overcome the usual levels of awareness and routine defenses.

As it turned out, my sister went through her routine with confidence and peace of mind. She trusted a parking lot security patrol to be there if necessary. She trusted other shoppers (some were in the next aisle) and the five lane traffic on John R Street to somehow protect her. She trusted her routine. Everything looked perfectly normal and non-threatening. Everything looked A-OK. Unfortunately, everything was not OK. My sister had never been told by anyone that her routine, with all of its sensible safety checks, was exactly what a rapist lurking nearby was expecting of her. She had never been told that a woman is usually most vulnerable to an attack when she least expects it. Rapists depend on a woman's predictability, her tendency to panic and the effective use of the element of surprise. A theme song from a once popular television program comes to mind.

When you least expect it, you're elected. You're the star today. Smile, you're on Candid Camera.
- Candid Camera Theme

My sister's plans for the evening came to a sudden halt when she unlocked her car door and attempted to enter. Someone suddenly grabbed her from behind in what is commonly called a bear hug. Both of the assailant's arms reached around her and were clasped together - forcefully pinning her arms close to her body. It was immediately apparent that whoever he was, she was no match. Without saying a word, he lifted her up, turned her sideways and attempted to throw her into his car which was parked next to hers. According to my sister, she was instantly paralyzed, overwhelmed and imprisoned with fear. Being "scared to death" suddenly took on a new meaning. She felt as if she were immediately experiencing the attack in someone else's body.

In a moment of time, she seemed to be immediately transported into a dream or a movie. "It was as if the attack was happening to my body, yet I wasn't completely there. I could not bring myself to grips with the fact that it (attack) was really happening." Her mind informed her that the attack was not real; his powerful grip convinced her otherwise.

My sister's first thought was to scream, but under the circumstances, screaming seemed impossible. She thought of fighting back, but fighting back was only a thought, far beyond what her body would agree to. The mental process was no longer the same. Everything had changed. An avalanche of thoughts, feelings and sensations, each indistinguishable and devastatingly confusing, bombarded her beyond belief.

She no longer breathed normally, but hyperventilated her way to light-headedness. Her legs weakened. Her entire mind and body weakened. According to my sister, "It was as if time was racing and yet standing still." Time didn't matter anyway. Someone helping her mattered. Screaming and fighting back mattered. Not getting raped mattered. Frozen with fear, my sister had no idea of what to do. Her attacker's plot was unfolding before her eyes - with or without her cooperation.

My sister was panicking and she didn't have a chance in the world of overcoming her predicament. In her state of panic, she did everything to defend herself that her mind and body allowed her to do - absolutely nothing. My sister did what you, dear reader, will probably do if ever attacked, if I cannot convince and motivate you to do otherwise.

Incidentally, my sister was not raped. Thank God for that. Her attacker accidentally bumped into and closed his opened car door. As he attempted to hold my sister and reopen the door, she fell away. He grabbed her hair and attempted to restrain her. Despite all of the confusion, my sister continued her momentum as she tumbled away from his grip.

She left her frustrated assailant standing there with a considerable part of her hair clenched in each fist. "I guess he didn't expect me to jerk away after he had a good piece of my hair." She didn't feel any pain from the hair pulling until afterward. She later described her loss of hair, bruises and wrenched arm as a small sacrifice to escape. The assailant fled.

Other shoppers, who my sister was sure must have seen the attack, did not intervene or offer information afterward. My sister ran toward the store entrance. "I must have been hysterical. When I entered the store, someone near a spiral clothes rack walked up and asked if I was all right. I told him to get help." The store security arrived and tried to comfort my sister. Moments later, Troy police officers were on the scene. My sister looked in a mirror and realized how the person who first asked whether she needed help knew she was in trouble. Her face was broken out with hives, most of her hair was disheveled; part of it was missing.

While the Troy police officers were filling out a report, the store security returned with my sister's purse and a bundle of hair. Fortunately, nothing was missing from the purse. My sister was unable to identify the suspect. After a few weeks, she received a call from the Oakland County prosecutor's office. They said a journal had been confiscated from a recently apprehended rape suspect. Information in the journal led the prosecutor's office to my sister.

She was apparently one of his last entries.

The prosecutor's office contacted my sister because the suspect had compiled some biographical information. He had written down my sister's license plate number and a description of her car. He had also inserted a description of thoughts and feelings which he must have been experiencing. The suspect had documented his stalking maneuvers. The man (I use the term loosely) had done his homework. I believe that most rapists do.

Besides, empirical data concerning premeditated and planned rape is difficult to find since rapists themselves are difficult to study. Most rapes go unreported and most rapists are never identified, apprehended or convicted. The offenders of the "silent" crime are mystery men.

Of the many entries in the book (more than twenty), six women came forward to testify.

My sister visited the trial to get a look at her attacker. He looked to be about six feet - four inches tall, husky and surprisingly good-looking. Other victims at the trial noticed that he had shaved off his mustache. My sister simply wanted to look into the face of the man who terrorized her. She wanted to see the rapist who nearly ruined her life. The assailant was sentenced to life in prison for the commission of several sexual assaults.

Place my sister's trauma somewhere back in your mind and remember the following. You are most vulnerable to an attack when you least expect one. Remember also, that if you have no idea of what to do, or cannot do it, chances are, you too will experience terror with a capital T. The good news is that there are other options. Two more chapters remain before introducing information which is designed to help you avoid and overcome such confrontations.

In this chapter, I have chosen an interview with a woman who was raped by an acquaintance. This is to shed some light on how detrimental the state of panic can be. We will also look at influencing factors. We will see how all of this applies to a horrendous problem in this country, the one commonly called date or acquaintance rape. We all have heard the cries of victimized women echoing from college campuses all over the country. Time and People magazines have displayed acquaintance/ date rape victims on their front covers. Much was said on what happened, but unfortunately little was written on how to prevent it. It is a sad state of affairs when television programs reveal how some college students have gone as far as writing on bathroom walls the names of known rapists in an attempt to warn others. Television programs, news papers, movies, etc. have all described incidents involving women who were raped by the boy next door, plumber, gas meter reader, salesman, teacher, fiancee, Uncle Bob, bell boy, lawn service representative, doctor, blind date, psychologist, police officer, husband, ex-husband, father, stepfather, brother, social worker and a long list of others. No wonder it is so difficult to profile a typical rapist. He can be anyone, anytime, anywhere.

I first met Madelyn at a UAW-Chrysler assembly plant in Warren, Michigan in August 1991. She represented a local college which was recruiting students in the area. She seemed highly motivated, enthusiastic, remarkably happy and well adjusted. After discussing our full-time positions with training companies, she asked if I had any additional professional interests. I shared with her the fact that since 1985, I had been lecturing and presenting rape prevention seminars for women. Concerning the UAW plants, my focus was limited to general self-defense for men and women. Unfortunately, the automotive plants were populated by few women; therefore, a dedicated rape-prevention program was out of the question. She immediately expressed an interest in the content of the book. As I outlined the general theme, she began to have a look in her eyes that I'm gradually learning to recognize. Her countenance began to telegraph an "it happened to me" appearance. It is difficult for me to describe this look, but when it is there, I know it. You don't have to be a clinical psychologist to make such an observation. Something had happened. She told me to my complete expectation that she had been raped. My response is always the same. I'm usually speechless as if a friend just told me that a loved one had died. Although by trial and error, I have learned to say some comforting things. I usually spend most of the time listening with my ears and with my heart.

Chapter Three - MADELYN

She began to reveal some startling details as if a confession was necessary. Pain and hurt which I had not noticed initially was written all over her face. She wanted to share her story. She wanted somebody to listen and know that what happened to her on an evening ten years earlier was not just another day. For her, it was the day that the earth stood still. As Madelyn talked, I did everything possible to convince her that none of her words were falling on deaf ears. I nodded, shook by head in disgust, sighed and commented on the horror of it all. I wanted her to know unconditionally - that I was in her corner.

She remarked that she would be willing to share her experience with me provided the interview would be used in the book or in my rape prevention seminars. This is exactly what I have done. Following is a telephone conversation between Madelyn and myself. I asked her to avoid sharing intimate sexual details. Her words, as accurately as I could record them within the time I had, are written below. Words of comfort which I shared with her will be mentioned in another chapter.

Q. Madelyn, let's go back to the beginning if you don't mind. How old were you when the attack took place? What were you like then?

A. I was 19 years old, almost twenty. Well, for one thing, I was still a virgin, which made things even worse. I guess you could say that I was attractive and pretty. At least, that's what everyone told me. I had a lot of friends - close friends. I was built really well. I was 38-24-35 - really busty. I didn't go out with that many guys. Some guys would always tell me on a date that they thought that I was a little too pretty for them. I didn't play hard-to-get as far as going out with somebody; I was just so insecure.

Q. It sounds to me like everything was OK for you back then.

A. I guess so, but I did have kind of a self-esteem problem, but so did most of my friends. I liked who I was though.

Q. Did you know the man who raped you?

A. Oh yeah, I knew him all right. That's the whole problem. I knew him, and I knew what he was like. I should have known better. I was so stupid. That's one thing that I forgot to tell you about myself back then. I did do some really dumb things.

Q. We're all guilty of that Madelyn. No one bats a thousand. No one. So, you knew this guy - right?

A. He was a lot older than me. I think he was about 28. His

name was Mark. My mother thought he looked like Charles Manson. I thought he was cute. He had a really big smile, brown eyes and dark, curly hair. Most women would be attracted to him. He was a furniture mover - strong and muscular.

Q. Where did you first meet him?

A. He was painting a house for a neighbor down the street. I knew the woman who lived there. I was the neighborhood babysitter. I knew just about everybody. While I was walking by her house, she asked me to stop by. When I went into her kitchen, I met Mark. We sat around the kitchen table talking. She kept hinting to Mark that someone needed to show this girl a good time. A good time for me was cruising through a McDonald's. The following week, Mark found out where I lived and asked me out. Against my mom's wishes and I guess my own conscience, I went out with him anyway. It was neat being asked out by an older guy. We went to a Mexican restaurant and then to see Star Wars. After the movie, we went to his parent's house. His mother thought that I looked so young. She didn't say it with the best tone of voice.

Q. So, that was your first date?

A. I wish. We were at his parent's house, sitting on the couch, and here's this guy - all over me. The most that I had ever done was kiss a boy and here's this guy acting like an animal. I said, "No way, you're crazy. Take me home." I started crying. I should have just walked home. He didn't try anything else.

Q. Mary, it sounds like this guy was trouble and you knew that. Did you try to stay away from him?

A. Oh, I tried. He kept driving by my house and he would always pull his car up to me when I was walking and apologize. I kept telling him that he was too old for me and that I wasn't ready to get serious with anybody. He even tried to convince my mother that he was a nice guy. He didn't convince her.

Q. So, then what?

A. I always kept a diary. I still have it. The problem is that my mother found it. She thought that I had sex with Mark. She wanted an explanation. I didn't have one. My mother continued to push and pull. It was time for a change. I moved in with a girlfriend of mine. She had her own apartment. She was raising her two year old son by herself.

Q. So you're on your own living with a friend. What next?

A. Everything was great. I watched the two year old and I had a great place to stay. But who do you think showed up? I couldn't believe it. Mark showed up out of the blue. To this day, I do not know how he found out where I lived.

Q. That must have been a shock. How did you react?

A. When I answered the door, the last person I expected to see was him. But there he was. He acted really nice - just like he did when he used to try to apologize to me. I was so stupid. I should have known better, but I guess I didn't. I felt safer in the apartment than I did at his parent's place. I let him come in. The baby was in the other room and my friend was coming home later. I felt like taking a little chance because he did have a really good side. I don't know why I let him in. It just happened.

Q. When did you sense that "Oh, oh, I've got a problem here?"

A. He came in and I told him he could sit on the couch. I was watching TV. We talked and joked around for quite a while. I could tell that he had been drinking. I drank a little with him, but I wasn't drunk or anything. I had mixed feelings about the whole thing. But he was fun to be with. I wasn't dressed that great. I had a wrapper on. To me, it covered me up more than a lot of other things that I wore. I guess to him it might have looked kind of sexy since it was all that I had on. He probably thought that I just came out of the shower. I didn't really have much on, but I didn't expect company either. I should have changed.

Q. Madelyn, you mentioned that you had mixed feelings when he first came in. I can understand that. Were things getting better or worse?

A. The one time I thought he was up to his old games again is when he couldn't believe that I was still a virgin. I honestly can't remember how we had discussed that before. I probably told him that or gave him that impression at his parents' house. He kept joking about how he just didn't know how he was supposed to treat a virgin. I didn't get any other indicators about what was going to happen. It just happened.

Chapter Three - MADELYN

Q. That's when he raped you?

A. He did more than rape me. He hurt me. He grabbed me and wrestled me to the floor. I didn't even have time to scream. I think I tried to scream. He had his hand over my mouth and was pulling off my wrapper. I couldn't believe it was happening. I was struggling, but he was winning. I kept thinking, "No, no, no - don't, don't, don't." I know he heard me say that too. When I got too loud, he would put his hand over my mouth. He kept saying "Shh, I love you. What are you crying about?" I was crying like crazy. He didn't care. He wanted what he wanted. I wasn't ready. It was really painful. It hurt more than I thought that it would. I kept crying and telling him that he was hurting me. I was bleeding all over the place. In fact, I bled for two weeks after that. He ripped me open. I was so embarrassed and shocked. I couldn't believe that it was all happening. I couldn't tell you how long everything took. It seemed like forever. He kept saying, "I finally had my little virgin." I hated him like I never hated anything before. I was sick to my stomach. He went into the bathroom and looked at himself. The way he was talking, it sounded like he was proud of all the blood. He came back into the living room and passed out next to me. I don't know why I didn't scream for help then. I was just lying there in shock. I was numb. I was lucky he didn't try and rape me again. It's funny, but I was thinking that maybe he was right - I deserved it. I should have known better. I hated him. I hated me. I hated everything that happened.

Q. Madelyn, you mentioned that he passed out. Did you think of calling the police or calling for help? Did you think about hurting him when you had the chance?

A. I didn't do anything. Can you believe it - nothing! I didn't want to do anything except take a hot shower. I had blood all over. I just about scalded myself. I was in the shower forever. I got some clean clothes on. I didn't want to go back in the living room until my girlfriend came home. She finally came home and saw him lying on the floor. She joked about me being with someone (sexually), since everybody always said that I was so innocent. Well, I wasn't innocent anymore. I stayed in the kitchen until he woke up. I asked him, "How could you do that to me?" I started crying. I think my friend heard me. All that he said was, "If I didn't, somebody else would have." I yelled at him and told him to get out. My girlfriend came in to see what was going on. I think he got scared and took off. I didn't tell her what happened. It was too late.

Q. *Madelyn, you kept this a secret then?*

A. I never would have told my dad. He once told me that there were three types of women. He would say "You're either somebody's wife, a virgin or a whore." When I finally got the nerve to tell my mom, I couldn't believe what she told me. She said, "Some guys are like that. They're a little too rough." "Too rough," I thought. "The guy ripped me open." Both of my parents believed that once you're together, you stay together.

Q. *What a mess. You didn't have anyone to turn to did you? Was that the end of it?*

A. No way. I saw him a week later. I started seeing him again. I know that's hard to believe. It's like I was brainwashed. He threatened to tell everybody what happened in his version. Can you believe that? He knew I wanted the whole thing to just go away. He took advantage of me for over five months. The sex was always painful. I thought that maybe - that's the way it was supposed to be. The only thing that scared him off was when I got pregnant. I have a ten year old boy from him

now. In fact, his birthday is coming up.

Except for a few words of comfort and support, the interview with Madelyn was concluded at this point. Madelyn did mention that she was seeing a therapist.

Frankly, I never had any difficulty believing Madelyn's account of what happened to her ten years ago. My only difficulty was in understanding how it could all take place.

Here was a young woman that was viciously raped, and due to the circumstances surrounding the ordeal, chose to tell no one. According to Madelyn, except for her mother, a therapist and myself, no one ever knew what happened to her.

I have heard or read dozens of such testimonials from women. Some, like Madelyn's, are more extreme than others. Without exception however, the same social conditioning, guilt, shame, anger, depression, confusion, fears, circumstantial entrapment, lack of a planned defense, etc., are mentioned repeatedly. Rape has been called the "all-American crime" (Griffin, 1971). "Its roots are firmly planted in the culture, nurtured by myths and taboos about gender and reinforced by pervasive stereotypes" (McCall's, May 1990). That description is especially true when it comes to date or acquaintance rape. Most of the women who informed me they had been raped by someone they knew, said that their rape was one of their best kept secrets.

"You can take better care of your secret than another can."
- Emerson

Consider Madelyn's predicament had she decided to report the crime and press charges. A defense attorney would have had a field day with the circumstantial evidence. The following questions would have been raised in a court of law:

• Why did she let Mark enter the apartment if he was so aggressive on their first social outing?

• Considering the fact that she was scantily dressed in a "wraparound", did it ever occur to her that their drinking, kissing and hugging, were leading toward a sexual encounter. It was obviously already very "sexual."

• Why didn't she attempt to scream for help?

• Why didn't she run or call for help when he passed out?

• Why didn't she inform her roommate what had happened?

• Why, why, why . . .

Madelyn's anticipated courtroom interrogation, her parent's lack of understanding and support and her social conditioning had her convinced that "she should have known better and deserved what she got." It was simply too much for this nineteen year old to bear.

She, like most women in this country, had been raised to be a victim. Loose laws, lenient sentencing and permissive parole boards allow sexual offenders the opportunity to roam the streets seeking whom they may devour. For a graphic illustration of this, read the article "Freed to Rape Again" in the October 1991 issue of Reader's Digest.

Criminals usually weigh the amount of profit against the amount of risk. It is not surprising then, that rapists perceive few deterrents in their quest. Consider the following information contained in I Never Called it Rape by Robin Warshaw (1988). The book contains a nationwide survey conducted on 32 college campuses by Ms. magazine, psychologist Mary P. Koss and the National Institute for Mental Health. The study revealed that:

• 1 in 4 women surveyed were victims of rape or attempted rape.

• 57 percent of the rapes occurred on dates.

• 84 percent of the women raped knew their attacker.

• Over 50 percent of the 3,187 female students experienced some form of sexual abuse.

• About 75 percent of the men and at least 55 percent of the women had been taking drugs or drinking prior to the attack.

In my seminars, I always remind parents sending their daughters off to some college campus that some form of rape prevention training should precede their academic studies.

College campuses place women in an environment which is extremely conducive to a high incidence of acquaintance rape. Typically, a lack of security officers and/or equipment, party-like atmosphere in dormitories and the amount of dating contribute to this horrendous problem.

Simply put, when it comes to date or acquaintance rape, a woman is usually alone with a person(s) who, she soon realizes, has more on his mind than a cup of coffee. A victim is forced to deal with the "I can't believe he is doing this" before directly con-fronting him defensively. The situation becomes more intense and so does her fear.

More often than not, she panics. And once she panics, the odds of avoiding rape weigh heavily against her. Her acquaintance meanwhile is probably aware that few women report such attacks, and if so, the conviction rate and sentencing are not necessarily anything to be too concerned about. Our society needs to come to grips with the dilemma facing women when their "no" just isn't enough.

In the next chapter, the questions from the General Awareness category in chapter one will be answered. Also, statistics compiled from several sources will be presented to shed additional light on the current rape epidemic in this country.

I will never forget the words spoken to me by an economics professor in 1972. After working a 12 hour shift in an ear deafening and mind deadening factory and sliding over icy streets for twenty minutes, there I sat in a college classroom listening to someone who apparently had made a decision to teach economics and learn English simultaneously. To make matters worse, my graded test was returned to me with a heart-stopping C+ written much too noticeably in red ink. I sipped some vending machine imitation coffee and stared in disbelief at the grade thinking about how economics was out and depression was in. I had worried about the test and studied my brains out preparing for it. I didn't have the foggiest notion of how to bring the grade up. The professor must have read my mind when he stated, "Some of you have not done as well as you would have liked." I felt like standing up and taking a bow. "You have learned an important lesson however. You now know what I expect on tests. Now you know what to be aware of." Essentially, he was telling me to not get discouraged, but to get concerned.

Despite the odds weighing heavily against any academic success, I decided to take his advice. I aced the second test. He was not attempting to discourage me; I already was. He had cautioned me in such a way as to encourage me. His point was well taken. I needed a proper awareness. And when it comes to rape prevention, so do you.

DON'T GET DISCOURAGED, GET CONCERNED.

How aware you are of something which is potentially dangerous, can significantly affect the likelihood of your avoiding and defending against it. That is precisely why I chose to begin this book with twenty questions which test your general awareness concerning the crime of rape. Following are the same questions with answers and/or comments pertinent to each:

1. What is your definition of rape? What actions would constitute rape in your mind?

I have not offered a definition of rape in this book for a specific reason. My definition does not amount to a hill of beans. It is your definition that matters. A man fondling you against your will can justifiably constitute rape in your mind. Perhaps, a man forcibly kissing you is all the "rape" that you can handle.

Researchers on the subject seem to agree that rape is not limited to sexual gratification nor is it necessarily sexually motivated. Dr. Judith Fein offers an interesting definition. "Rape is a violent assault. Rape is an aggression committed under force or the threat of force upon an unconsenting person." (Fein, 1988, pp. 1, 10). Rape involves more than mere sexuality; anger and power are integral components as well (Groth, 1979, p. 13). A pamphlet distributed by the Troy Police Department (the city where my sister was attacked) says that "Rape is a crime of violence, not a crime of passion. It can happen to you."

Personally, I am not comfortable with a definition of rape which simply places it under the general category of violence and downplays the sexual emphasis. I have met women who have had their jaw or nose broken due to a physical assault. It was obvious that their assaults severely traumatized them. There was also evidence of physical and psychological recovery.

On the other hand, women who have been raped have received much more than a fractured bone or bruise. The actual rape itself may only be the beginning of their problems. The aftermath often continues for months, years, and for some women - forever. Guilt, shame and a sense of total violation and exposure create deep wounds within each victim, wounds which heal so very slowly and painfully. The sexual violation involved in a rape transcends the physical and psychological trauma produced by other forms of physical abuse. I refuse to water it down.

Rapists do not earn their title by repeatedly striking their victims in the face; they sexually abuse them. I doubt that there is a woman alive who "defines" her rape as a physical assault committed by a violent assailant who was simply releasing his rage and attempting to control. The trauma is immeasurable and the assailant is usually viewed as something subhuman.

2. What do you think is the legal definition of rape?

According to the Bureau of Justice Statistics, U.S. Department of Justice, rape is "carnal knowledge through the use of force or the threat of force, including attempts" (BJS, p. 7).

Many states define rape as undesired vaginal intercourse between male and female, but usually also include anal intercourse, fellatio, and cunnilingus between persons regardless of sex. Many states have followed the lead of Michigan by modifying their rape laws so that "sexual contact" becomes the central focus, not simply penetration. Generic terms such as "actor" and "victim" replaced "male" and "female." An "actor" can no longer force sexual contact on a "victim" without risking prosecution for some offense. Prior to 1975, Michigan's rape laws failed to adequately punish offenders who forced sexual contact. Most offenses could fall under simple assault and battery. Marital rape, use of objects for penetration, and a woman's sexual history are some issues which legislatures have been forced to come to grips with. Your local library will have information available to you which clearly defines what constitutes rape or sexual conduct in your state.

3. How many rapes were reported (documented) in 1990?

Whenever conducting seminars on rape prevention, I always made it a point to ask participants to raise their hand if they personally knew someone who had been raped. Between one-third and one-half of the hands would be raised. Frankly, it served as my personal index on the rape problem in this country. The show of hands increased both the intensity of my speaking and the listening of the audience.

The Uniform Crime Report compiled by the Federal Bureau of Investigation is a good source for such information. This nationwide statistical effort incorporates the services of approximately 16,000 state, county and city law enforcement agencies. The report's estimate of rapes committed in the United States in 1990 was 102,555. According to a 1990 Senate Judiciary report, police agencies reported 100,433 rapes in 1990. That equals nearly 300 women raped every day of the year. A staggering 6,983 rapes were reported in my home state of Michigan in 1990.

4. Our federal government annually estimates the number of rape victims. Take a guess at what that number was for 1990? What do you think the annual estimate was between 1973 and 1987?

The Bureau of Justice Statistics (BJS) reports in its publication Victims of Violent Crime (1991), the Bureau of Justice Statistics (BJS) estimated that 155,000 women were raped annually between 1973 and 1987. That is well over two million victims. Even if they are only batting 50% in their estimates, that is still over one million women ravaged by rape. Since more then 500,000 women were interviewed to compile the statistics, the estimates are probably accurate.

Some estimate that between 1/3 and 1/5 of the women in the United States over the age of 12 will be the victim of rape or an attempted rape.

After analyzing several independent studies on the prevalence of rape, Mary Koss concluded that rape studies "greatly expand the scope of rape beyond the reported crime statistics and estimates of unreported crime derived from independent studies." According to the studies, Koss reports that:

- 20-40 percent of women report at least one episode of sexual abuse as children.

- Approximately 30 percent of high school and post secondary students report that they experienced either rape or attempted rape.

- Approximately 44 percent of adult women have experienced some form of serious sexual assault (Koss, pp. 9,10).

Every independent study I have read has shown that the crime of rape is not the rarity which perhaps you have been led to believe. My contention is that the crime is wide spread and much worse than what women have been told. Rape, in my mind, is one of the best kept secrets by American women.

5. What percentage of rapes is reported to police departments?

Most estimates suggest that for every reported rape, three to ten unreported rapes occur. The June 3, 1991 issue of Time magazine has a picture of Katie Koestner, a rape victim, on the front cover. Eight pages of that issue are dedicated to the subject of rape. Readers are informed that "The experts guess - that's all they can do under the circumstances - less than 10% (of rape victims) will report the assault."

6. Why do you think women are reluctant to report being raped?

According to the BJS (1991), common reasons for refraining from reporting rape include:

- They considered the rape to be a personal or private matter which they wanted to resolve personally.

- They feared some type of reprisal by the rapist, his family or friends.

- They feared that the police would be insensitive toward them and ineffective in resolving the matter.

- They did not believe that sufficient proof was available.

Another reason contributing to the reluctance of women to report their attack is the grueling courtroom proceedings required for prosecution. The recent and well publicized trials involving William Kennedy Smith, Mike Tyson and at the time, Supreme Court nominee Clarence Thomas showed how stressful courtroom proceedings can be for female (alleged) victims. Television movies and motion pictures such as The Accused have graphically illustrated for women the trauma experienced by women who seek justice via the court system. The courtroom ordeal, even when the sexual offender is found guilty, can be an embarrassing, frustrating and frightening experience for the victim.

7. In 1990 how well did the United States protect its women from rape as compared to other nations?

According to the Senate Judiciary Committee (1991), the United States led the world in reported rapes.

The U.S. rape rate was:

- 8 times higher than in France.

- 15 times higher than in England.

- 23 times higher than in Italy
- 26 times higher than in Japan.

The United States is the most violent and self-destructive nation on Earth.
- Senate Judiciary Committee

Note: Answers for questions 8 through 16 were provided by the Bureau of Justice Statistics, U. S. Department of Justice.

8. Where do most rapes generally occur?

Most rapes take place at home.

- 4 in 10 rapes took place at home.
- 2 in 10 occurred at or near a friend's home.
- 2 in 10 occurred on the street.

9. When do most rapes occur?

- Two-thirds of the rapes occurred at night.

Note: Remember approximately one-third of the women were raped during the day. Never, never, completely let your guard down.

10. Between what ages are most women raped?

Women age 16 to 24 are three times more likely to be raped than other women.

11. How old do you think the average rapist is?

Nearly three-fourths of all rapists are over the age of 21. Most are between the ages of 21 and 29.

12. What race of women is more likely to be raped than others?

As a percentage, black women were significantly more likely to be raped than others. In absolute numbers, more white women were raped than other races.

13. Are most offenders armed with a weapon when committing rape?

Most (75%) are unarmed.

14. What is the likelihood of a woman being raped if she physically resists with self-protection measures?

71% of the women who physically resisted were **not** victims of a completed rape.

15. What is the likelihood of a woman being injured if physically resisting?

- 58% of the victims who resisted were injured.
- 46% of the victims who did not resist were injured.

Note: It seems to me that you might as well put up a fight since there is a strong probability that you will be injured anyway.

16. What is the average length of a rapist's sentence and what part of it is usually served in prison or jail?

- Median sentence: 5 years and 6 months
- Median time served: 2 years and 2 months

17. Rapists typically have several advantages over their victims. Can you name at least five? Which one is most advantageous?

- Element of surprise

- Size and strength

- Presence of a weapon

- More than one rapist

- Planned and practiced attack

- More than one attacker

- Low risk of being arrested and convicted

- More physically aggressive

- Tendency of the victim to panic

(This last advantage is my choice for the most advantageous award)

18. Can you name three things which offenders usually fear when committing rape?

- An audience

- Surprises

- The initial attack taking too long, in effect, not gaining control quickly enough

19. When do you think you are usually most vulnerable to a rapist's attack?

You are most vulnerable to an attack when you least expect it. Why? There is a tendency to let your guard down.

20. Name five parts of the body where a rapist is particularly vulnerable to an attack or strike. What would be your primary target?

- Groin

- Throat

- Eyes

- Nose

- Solar Plexus

- Ribs

- Knees (My choice for primary target)

This chapter was not written to frighten you into a siege mentality of paranoia and discouragement. The fear of being raped probably raises its ugly head often enough. I simply wanted to caution you.

DON'T GET DISCOURAGED, GET CONCERNED.

No woman is completely defenseless because no rapist is completely invincible. He cannot make contact with a victim without exposing his own vulnerable body parts. Similarly, since he sometimes "socially interacts" with his victim, he exposes himself to verbal and psychological defeat as well. To avoid putting the cart before the horse, it makes sense to first explain a rapist's vulnerabilities. Then, I'll introduce techniques and strategies which are designed to exploit them. I'll give you some items to think about, some things that will become valuable ammunition.

PSYCHOLOGICAL VULNERABILITY

Audiences

If there is one thing on this earth that a rapist does not want, it is an audience. A rapist either looks for a victim in an isolated area or abducts her from a public area and transports her to one. He is generally confident and prepared to confront his victim, but unexpected visitors are entirely out of the question. A safe and controlled environment is an absolute must for a rapist. Neighbors, friends, relatives, crowds, etc., bring with them challenges which are unpredictable and difficult for him to deal with. Where the idea of being raped frightens you, the fear of getting caught in the act frightens the rapist. A rapist's fantasy simply does not have a "Public Welcome" sign anywhere in the area. He usually will attempt to do things with a woman, which under normal and casual circumstances, would be unthinkable by him and his victim. His little plot has been concocted somewhere back in his twisted mind. Unfortunately, he is continually seeking victims to write into the script. Only victims are invited to audition; others are not. He cannot risk it. The plot will not unfold; it will not work. Therefore, everything that you do in your attempt to defend against a rapist must include drawing the attention of others to your predicament. If a rapist is attempting to draw you away from others, he is trying to get you to an environment which is rapist friendly. Don't let it happen. Never go from point A to point B. Do not let him set the stage. It only makes sense that he will be more apt to rape and injure you in an area where he has complete, uninterrupted control of the situation.

Lack of Control

A rapist knows that he must be in complete control for you to comply with, and to satisfy, his wishes. Since rape involves power, anger and sex, he will attempt to dictate and control all actions. He makes up the rules. His estimate of your resistance and general predictability is what he is prepared to challenge and to overcome. Any variance or deviation from his expectations creates temporary obstacles. He must then improvise and adapt. These require thought, energy and time. Time he spends reacting to your actions is less time available for him to rape you. The old street phrase "Slam, bam, thank you ma'am" is applicable to a rapist's time table. He knows that you are most vulnerable to an attack when panicking and shocked by the sudden violence or threat of violence. Therefore, he knows that he must quickly gain complete control of you before you have enough time to regroup and defend. When you are in shock and "numbed," he knows your defense is probably at its weakest point. On the other hand, when he loses control, he feels vulnerable. **When he feels vulnerable, he is.** You must quickly convince him that the attack is not going to happen according to his plan. He must be convinced that the rape is not going to happen, period.

Verbal Inferiority

In teaching men, women and children self-defense, I have always taught students to avoid being entrapped by an individual who is trying to verbally intimidate them. Generally, a "bully" usually establishes an edge by verbally threatening a victim. He will usually dominate in the verbal arena and will then confidently consider physical abuse as well. While observing my children and others, I have always marveled how quickly they learn to verbally intimidate one another. Once the aggressive child detects an iota of fear or a lack of resistance in the other child, this usually serves as a green light to increase the aggression. As children grow older, the verbal intimidation becomes more creative and forceful. I have met some people whom I would label as master intimidators. Although some of them had a physical presence which demanded a certain level of respect, others did just fine using their mouths. Examples of some creative lines used over the years include:

"You talking to me?" I don't see anyone else standing here. You better not be talking to me."

"I'm going to knock you into yesterday."

"If I want your opinion, I'll beat it out of you."

Rapists have been known to blurt out a few lines to frighten and control their victims.

"Do what I say and nothing will happen to you. Act up and I'll cut your throat."

"I've killed other women who didn't listen to me. Don't think I won't hurt you."

"You can do what I say, or else I will have to make all of this real painful. It's up to you."

"I can get real crazy. I am crazy. You give me any problems and I'll do things to you that you won't believe."

"You open your mouth and tell anybody what happened

here, I'll find you before they (police) find me. If the police start looking for me, I'll have nothing to lose. I'll make sure you don't talk."

"Don't say anything to anybody and I won't go after you, open your mouth and I'll get one of your kids. You can run but you can't hide."

"No one will believe you. I'll bring up some stuff up that will convince them that you're not the little Miss Good Girl that they think. I'll deny it. It will be your word against mine."

"Remember that I know where you live and it's only a matter of time before I find out where your kids go to school."

I have always taught students to avoid doing battle verbally. Too often, victims are drawn into a verbal confrontation and as a result fail to concentrate on physically defending themselves. Since verbal contests usually occur at close range, they do nothing more than place victims in jeopardy.

Rapists often verbally threaten and taunt their victims first and then they proceed to instruct. Anything which he says will be used to terrorize and force his victim into submission. Later statements, questions, etc. will be used to taunt, embarrass and humiliate. What he cannot afford to do is struggle or lose in the verbal arena. If his statements do not threaten and if his words do not control, he

has to adjust. He must go to a plan B. Although it is true that he may have to become more physical, he may not be prepared or willing to do that. If his verbal approach does not work, he has lost the first round. Losing the first round is never an ideal start for anybody.

If you decide to verbally communicate, then concentrate on using direct and assertive statements. They are more effective than those interpreted as weak and pleading. Compare the following statements. Think about which ones would enable a rapist to feel in control of the situation and therefore confident of carrying out a successful attack.

"Please don't. I'm a virgin." or "Get your hands off me."

"Please don't do this to me." or "Don't even think about it."

"How can you do this?" or "You will not get away with this."

"Why are you doing this?" or "This is rape. You are going to prison if you don't stop."

Surprises

Women I have questioned have left me with the impression that a vast majority of them have made identical efforts in the area of rape prevention. So do I believe that most rapists have stereotyped their victims? You bet your life. If most women have traditionally reacted to a rapist's attack in much the same way, and if everything being taught to women as rape-prevention techniques is common knowledge, most rapists will know what to expect and, therefore, what to do.

Remember my sister's parking lot routine. After selecting, stalking, studying and stereotyping their victims, rapists then set out to control the attack from beginning to end. They can generally choose their victim and then decide the time, place, severity, length and nature of the attack. Everything usually goes along as planned. Think about that. Think about what you can change. Think about what he is not prepared for. He is not prepared for any surprises. Any tricks up your sleeve or in your pocket can rattle him to his bootstraps. I heard an old saying that suggests "Cunning and wisdom will always prevail over strength and vigor." Women need to learn how to surprise their attacker so that his first thought will be "For crying out loud, what in the world is she going to do next . . . ". Surprise him and he must think, hesitate and weigh the odds. This buys you precious time and significantly increases your chances of avoiding rape. Think about it. Be creative.

PHYSICAL VULNERABILITY

Few would question the fact that most rapists have several physical advantages over their victims. Rapists are usually larger, stronger, and more experienced when it comes to physical confrontations. A weapon can be in the hand of a rapist whereas an unsuspecting victim may have nothing more than a bath towel. A rapist's body may be performing optimally due to an adrenaline charge activated from anger, rage or lust. A victim on the other hand, may be frozen with fear. Again, it sounds as if the deck is stacked doesn't it. Well, it is. All the rules seem to favor Goliath. So what do you do? You change the rules. You don't hit him where he is protected and invincible. On the contrary, you hit him where it hurts and where he is weak. He is not the knight in shining armor that he thinks. He is not the bigger-than-life conqueror which he has set himself up to be. He has unprotected areas all over his body and he cannot come near a victim without exposing one or more of them. He is always risking something. You must decide what it is and how to attack it. If you see only his armor and attack only his armor, he risks nothing. Those are not the rules to play by. One of the first things that I learned as a martial artist was how to protect myself by maximizing my strengths and minimizing those of my opponent. I've learned as well how to protect my weaknesses and expose and attack his. To me, the martial arts have always been the great equalizer. An individual's lack of size, strength, anger, etc. against an opponent is compensated for by an ability to use different parts of the body effectively. Efficient body movement makes the difference.

Women who have practiced martial arts know that they do not have to concern themselves with matching an attacker pound for pound. They can use their legs, elbows, knees, head, hands, etc. to stun, injure and immobilize a much larger and stronger opponent. A woman who has developed an effective self defense system may be forced to defend herself against a rapist. Initially, she must take part in his little game, but fortunately, she does not have to play by his rules. She can make her own rules. If he is not prepared to deal with her repertoire of self-defense skills, he has his work cut out. She knows where he is vulnerable and that is exactly where she will focus her attack. She hits him where it hurts and concentrates on hurting him where she hits. If you are not a trained martial artist, chances are you have not been taught where and how to strike an assailant.

Let's look at where Mr. Rapist is physically vulnerable. The old saying "What you see is what you get" does not have to be swallowed hook, line and sinker. Either you have been socially conditioned to see insurmountable obstacles such as size or strength or you have been trained to spot physical vulnerabilities. When defending against a rapist, you do not

have to match him pound for pound or strength against strength. You resort to your bag of tricks.

BODY CHARTS

Knees

Professional football players prove an important point for me when it comes to teaching rape-prevention. On the field these well conditioned athletes are padded and protected from head to foot; at least that is the objective. I have always been amazed at how much physical punishment is passed around the playing field by these modern day gladiators. Some of these guys have taken jarring hits from other players, stood up and acted as if nothing really happened. However, occasionally a player is hit near the knees and then it is a different story. With enough impact to the knee, the player is no longer able to run, walk or sometimes even stand. Leg and knee injuries are a common sight on any football field. Why? There is no way to protect the knee from impact without inhibiting its functioning. When a knee that is supporting a 250 pound fullback is suddenly moved out of a balanced position, most of the weight will shift to a part of the knee that cannot withstand it. See Figures 5-1 and 5-2.

Something has to give. Tendons, cartilage, muscles and bones are overwhelmed and become damaged. The 250 pound

Chapter Five - HE IS VULNERABLE

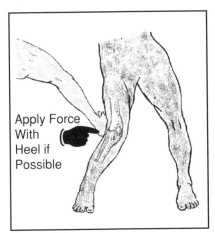

Apply Force With Heel if Possible

Figure 5-1

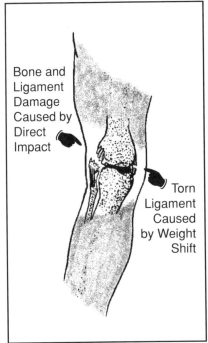

Bone and Ligament Damage Caused by Direct Impact

Torn Ligament Caused by Weight Shift

Figure 5-2

a man ever attempts to physically assault or rape you. Remember that a well-conditioned, padded and protected football player cannot withstand a sudden, well-focused and forceful blow to the knees. His only protection is to avoid getting hit in this area.

A rapist, no matter how big and strong, cannot come near you or stay near you without exposing one or both of his knees. His weight will be shifting from one knee to the other. He will probably be standing flatfooted. He is vulnerable to a kick in either knee. A kick directed to his knees, even if marginally executed, can inflict considerable damage. The kick can prove effective even if delivered slightly above or below the knee.

During sparring sessions with other martial artists, I have been accidentally kicked in the knees by beginning practitioners. Lower rank martial artists are notorious for kicking low due to a lack of flexibility and focus. Fortunately for me, my leg was not stationary and did not have much of my weight on it. High ranking martial artists have kicked toward my knees as well. Usually they knew that they would miss and therefore kicked forcefully. Some knew that they would make contact and therefore controlled the amount of thrust. Sometimes they made mistakes and I usually paid for them. Fortunately, I was never seriously hurt. The pain and

man is helped or carried off the field grimacing in pain. The injured player is history.

I encourage you to remember the preceding illustrations if

loss of balance did make me realize how vulnerable my knees were, even under controlled conditions.

After years of training, I finally overcame the fear of getting hit by an opponent, but the fear of a well-focused kick to my knees has never left me. Eventually, I got to the point where I refused to spar with anyone who would be allowed to throw kicks anywhere near the knees. One slight mistake could find me grimacing like the football player mentioned above.

Ultimately, you have to believe what I am telling you about a man's knees. They were designed for many reasons, not one of which is to get hit. By design, they cannot withstand the force that a woman can deliver with a properly executed kick. In teaching self-defense classes, I usually dwell a long time when it comes to techniques to the knees. They do not require as much balance, strength or flexibility as do other kicking techniques. If you ever kick a rapist in the knees (as illustrated in chapter 7), there is no question in my mind, he is going down. Like the fallen football player, he will be grimacing in pain.

Groin

I have asked many women what they would do to a man if they could only choose one physical technique to protect themselves. The number one response is a swift, hard kick to the groin. A groin kick is an excellent technique, but it does have some drawbacks. First, most men know to expect a kick to the groin and are usually prepared to defend against it. Second, the groin area is not as easy to kick as most people think. Third, a groin kick may not be enough to completely stop an attacker. Nevertheless, the groin is an extremely vulnerable area. Frederic Storaska does a fine job of describing this target. "The testicles are about the same consistency and strength as a ripe plum - without the pit. Any woman can squeeze one flat in a single motion" (Storaska, 1975, p. 99). I have never met or heard of any man who could withstand a sharp blow or squeezing of the testicles.

I have been kicked with considerable force in the groin area while wearing a protective cup. At the moment of impact, the pain was absolutely excruciating. Fortunately, I was not seriously injured. However, understand this, I was completely immobilized. The pain shot up from my groin into the abdominal area. Every second that passed after the impact scared me to death. I was afraid that the pain would increase. Any attempt to move my legs seemed to intensify the pain. It was a horrible experience.

When it comes to receiving a strike to the groin, there are no supermen. Several times I have been struck in the groin

Chapter Five - HE IS VULNERABLE

area while not wearing protective equipment except perhaps a jock strap (supporter). My opponents did not direct forceful blows to my groin to inflict damage, but merely focused a light technique. The pain was still there, particularly if the strike was delivered in a rising direction. The point that I am trying to drive home is that even a weak strike to this area can still immobilize an attacker. You can take that to the bank.

Throat

There are some men out there who have necks the size of some women's waists. A rapist may have strong trapeziums and sternocleidomastoid muscles to protect the sides of the neck; however, the front of the neck is entirely unprotected. Take your own finger and lightly poke yourself in different spots around the front of the neck in the throat area. Quite tender don't you think? The windpipe, commonly called the Adam's Apple, is easily damaged by a focused strike. When the windpipe if struck with sufficient force, it will collapse and totally incapacitate an assailant.

Eyes

Although scratching, poking or gouging an attacker's eyes can inflict pain and stop his attack, these techniques resemble the groin strike in that most rapists will not be surprised by your efforts. In the following chapter, the mechanics of an unusual

eye technique will be presented with surprising methods of delivery.

Nose

Anyone who has ever been hit hard in the nose will do almost anything to avoid having it happen again. The pain is intense. The eyes will immediately begin to water. To compound the problem, the nose usually bleeds easily and, if struck with enough force, bleeds profusely.

Hair

Pulling the hair hurts and it distracts. Pulling the hair does something else which is probably more important when it comes to rape prevention. Pulling the hair controls. Like a bit in a horse's mouth, pulling the hair controls the entire body and most of its movement.

Ribs

When someone is hit hard in the ribs, the first breath is an absolute nightmare. As you begin to breathe, you begin to feel a pain which is more pronounced than the initial strike. Movement of the ribs due to each breath is agonizing. You cannot move and you have a difficult time breathing.

When you learn how to focus a foot, knee or elbow to the ribs, an attacker will instantly think as Ronald Reagan once commented, "Frankly, I'd rather be in Philadelphia."

Solar Plexus/Xiphoid

Anyone who has taken a course in CPR has heard the term "xiphoid." It is at the bottom of the sternum and CPR students are instructed to avoid pushing on this area when attempting to compress the chest. This portion of the sternum can be easily damaged.

Directly below the xiphoid is the solar plexus. Webster's New World Dictionary defines the solar plexus as "a network of nerves in the abdominal cavity behind the stomach and in front of the uppermost part of the aorta, containing ganglia that send nerve impulses to the abdominal viscera." A second definition will please young readers of this book by describing the solar plexus as "the area of the belly just below the sternum, or breastbone."

The point is that this area is an excellent target since it is a nerve center. A hard thrust which penetrates the area underneath the xiphoid will "knock the wind out of" an assailant and momentarily shock his nervous system. A near miss which touches a lower rib or the xiphoid can stun him as well.

In the next chapter, a self-defense system which I have specifically developed for women will be introduced. This system is designed to exploit those vulnerabilities. By doing this, your chances of being raped are minimized and your ability to avoid and defend against it is strengthened. You need more than a few, common and well-known desperation techniques. You need what I refer to as Systematic Self-Defense.

Chapter Six - SYSTEMATIC SELF-DEFENSE

I like a story which Herbert E. Noe, my pastor once told during a sermon. A burdened church member went to a pastor for advice. The pastor's first question was, "How are things going for you?" The church member replied, "Not so good, under the circumstances." The pastor then wisely asked, "Well, what are you doing **under** the circumstances? Don't live life under the circumstances, rise above them." When it comes to rape prevention, I pose the same question to you. What are you doing under the circumstances?

For whatever reason, you have decided to read this book and have apparently made it this far. You have been asked to answer several questions. I have attempted to illustrate how traumatic a confrontation with a rapist can be and have asked you to remember the experiences of two women. I have asked you to look at statistical information in order to caution you. Now, I am asking you to make an important decision which I strongly suspect that most women in this country have not made. Decide to actively and proactively develop an effective rape prevention system now, so if ever needed, it will be there.

Options developed now will guarantee available options later. **A multitude of options is the best defense in the world.** Do something now. I like how Lisa Sliwa addresses the sub-ject of responsibility when it comes to protecting yourself. "You can blame men, your mother, rock videos and pornography for the increasing violence women face, and while you're pointing your finger, someone is going to grab your behind and try to knock you on the ground. You are thinking archaically unless you accept that fighting violence against women is your responsibility" (Sliwa, 1986, p. 51).

Perhaps you might be thinking, "Right . . . but you don't know how much I fear being raped. I would probably panic and faint. I never have been very physical, aggressive, etc." So what? Fear is necessary. All the training in the world cannot remove some degree of fear in life-threatening situations. Mohammed Ali was supposedly hypnotized before some of his boxing matches. I know one thing, his fear of getting hit was still there. My, how he ducked, bobbed and weaved his way out of the way of punches. He developed reflexes to accompany his fear of getting hit. Fear will be there. You simply need to develop a controlled confidence with which to confront it. This can make fear work for you rather than against you.

What is the best defense against a rapist who usually has a planned attack? A planned defense. Over the years, I have been taught by martial arts instructors to develop a series of defenses. This principle forces an opponent to deal with defensive barriers in stages. Similarly, police training I have received suggested that force needs to be met with equal and justifiable force. As an assailant's threatening behavior escalates, so should defensive action. A planned defense which increases in intensity as a threat escalates is both practical and effective. I have modified some of these teachings and have adapted them for women when it comes to defending against rape. My contention is that effective self-defense, particularly when it comes to rape prevention, offers options - a way out. I call this systematic self-defense. This system involves several steps which can generally be applied sequentially. The system encourages a woman to apply the five **D**'s for protection against rape.

- **D**iscern

- **D**istrust

- **D**istract

- **D**efend

- **D**epart

Situations can occur under which the systematic self-defense system cannot be fully applied. This repertoire of psychological and physical steps (techniques) can still be used in part to effectively defend against a rapist.

This system offers options which can be trusted and tried when confronted by a rapist. Options offer hope, something to believe in and to hold on to when the fear of being raped surfaces. Each step will be explained with examples of application.

DISCERN

Many women have said that prior to a rape, something told them to be careful and to beware. A still, small voice seemed to suggest that something was wrong - bad wrong. A gut feeling signaled danger ahead. The problem for most of the women was that they simply did not trust their intuition. They did not trust what they sensed and felt.

Often in acquaintance rapes, the offender's sexual advance is not perceived as the beginning of a rape. This can be difficult for many women to recognize. It seems that women in this country have been conditioned to expect a guy to try something sexual. Moreover, the guys are conditioned to go for it. Young people are taught through television, movies and their peers that "this is all part of growing up." A little sexual flirtation, taunting and teasing are all part of "making out."

The real problem lies in the fact that victims of acquaintance rape usually think that there is a way out. This is especially true if the sexual advance is only perceived as a "guy coming on a little bit too strong." They believe that the loose hands will slow down and that a simple

"No" will suffice. Well, sometimes the hands continue groping and NO! is not an acceptable answer.

The thought that "I can't believe he is doing this" must be dealt with immediately. Sometimes it isn't. Due to the "numbing" effect of the continued sexual advances, a victim's state of confusion can be interpreted as a moment of indecision. This moment of indecision can then be misinterpreted to fit the common male fantasy that "deep down, she really wants what I am attempting to do, and gradually she will be more than willing." The motion picture and television industry has glamorized this conquering of the prize.

It should be pointed out again that drugs and alcohol significantly contribute to the likelihood of a rape occurring. Granted, drugs and alcohol can dull the senses and lower inhibitions. This does not give offenders license to presume that the chemical influences are freeing up a woman's sexual inhibitions and desires. A woman, when under the influence of drugs, may do many things normally out of character for her. Some have mentioned walking on the roof of a house, giving an individual a "piece of her mind," and burying the speedometer on her car. Her fear and repulsive attitude toward being raped is still there, but due to the alcohol or drugs, lost and hidden behind her confused and distorted state of mind.

One of the most powerful things on earth is a woman's intuition. It is God-given and it is powerful. My recommendation for you is to learn to trust it. When confronted by someone whom you suspect or feel is a potential rapist, trust your senses. What if you're wrong and he turns out to be a real nice guy? So what? He will get over it and he will survive. On the other hand, if you sense, feel or suspect that someone is a rapist and choose to ignore, distrust or repress it, then you better hope he isn't. If he is, you may never get over it and you may not survive.

I am aware of the fact that certain situations, such as surprise attacks, can make discernment (as outlined below) quite difficult. Nevertheless, partial application can still frustrate, confuse and deter a rapist. My recommendation is for you to discern with your senses everything around you when the situation so requires. In police (reserve) administration training, I was taught to systematically assess the situation at hand and inform others of the status. The "situation" included the general vicinity, victims, assailants, criminal activity, etc. Proper discernment was essential to safeguard the safety of others and myself. Likewise, when attempting to avoid and defend against rape, proper discernment of a situation is necessary.

Chapter Six - SYSTEMATIC SELF-DEFENSE

This requires assessment of both the assailant and the general vicinity.

Assailant (rapist)

I have not profiled a "typical" rapist for the simple fact that I do not believe it can be done. Most of the available information on rapists is the result of studies involving incarcerated offenders. Consider the fact that most rapes go unreported and even fewer suspects are convicted. Research is therefore limited to the few who got caught and who are willing to undergo psychiatric testing and evaluation. They are hardly a representative sample.

After collaborating with Dr. Menachim Amir, Jean MacKellar described the typical rapist as "disturbingly ordinary." "The crime is most often committed by men who are young, poorly educated, and of the lowest social and economic groups. In the United States these offenders are predominantly black and frequently unemployed" (MacKellar, 1975, p. 68). Much has changed in our society since 1971 when Dr. Amir's Patterns in Forcible Rape was published. Don't think for a minute that you can pick out a rapist by way of simplistic stereotyping.

Every available study suggests that most rapes are committed by acquaintances. As a result, preconceived notions of what Ricky the Rapist looks like can be more trouble than they are worth. Since a rapist can be difficult to "identify," following are some guidelines to help you in detecting behavioral patterns and activities that could signal trouble.

Beware of:

- Someone who makes you feel uncomfortable. You might not be able to completely explain this "uneasiness," but if a gut feeling seems to suggest he is up to no good, act on that feeling. Trust your intuition.

- Obvious signs of drinking or drug usage. Often, rapists commit their crimes under the influence of drugs and/or alcohol.

- Repeated attempts, however subtle, to isolate you from the presence of others. Remember, rapists do not like audiences.

- A sudden onslaught of sexually explicit language or sexually aggressive advances which seem out of character for your friend or acquaintance.

- Be particularly cautious if your initial efforts to dissuade him are of no effect. If NO is not enough now to stop his early advances, then any effort to say NO later will probably fall on deaf ears.

If you have decided that an attack is eminent, assess and evaluate the "threatening" individual confronting you. As best as you can, attempt to learn if the assailant is:

- Armed with a weapon.

- Attempting to close the distance between himself and you.

- Exhibiting some form of emotional instability, rage, nervousness, etc.

- Physically overpowering and "in shape" enough to catch you should a means of escape become available.

Remember, if someone does not look "right" to you, he probably isn't.

Vicinity

You should always be aware of your surroundings, particularly when alone. If for some unforeseen reason, you find yourself stranded in what might be a threatening environment, attempt to:

- Summon the attention of others.

- Visualize where an assailant may be lurking such as behind bushes, under a stair well, behind or under a car, etc.

- Identify objects which can be used as a weapon.

- Look for escape routes.

When it comes to discerning a potentially dangerous situation, perhaps the most important statement for you to remember is that:

If a situation seems amiss and the probability of being raped seems to jump out at you, then redflag the situation. Prepare for war.

IT IS BETTER TO BE SAFE THAN TO BE SORRY.

DISTRUST

Once you have discerned that an individual may be intending to rape you, or if an individual has in some way verbally or physically communicated his intentions, be sure that you do not believe anything he says to calm your fears. He may tell you that you will not be hurt. He may order you into a bedroom with a promise that you will not be touched. Remember, a man contemplating committing rape will do anything to control the situation. Lying is high on the list. Trust your intuition more than any words coming out of his mouth.

My sister's parking lot experience illustrates the danger of placing too much trust that others will protect you from being raped. Don't rely on anyone who attempts to assure you that the likelihood of a rape occurring is small. Based on reported rapes alone, there is sufficient reason to challenge such a statement. I believe that if the actual number of women raped by strangers and acquaintances was somehow revealed, no one in their right mind would dare tell you as a woman, "Don't worry about it." Distrust anyone who attempts to persuade you to lower your guard.

Chapter Six - SYSTEMATIC SELF-DEFENSE

DISTRACT

Once you have discerned that an individual is a potential threat, and have no desire at all to trust him, you need to distract him as quickly as possible. You have to convince him that the rape is not going down the way he might think. You have to find a way to sidetrack him and disrupt the plot which he sees unfolding before his eyes.

Distracting him can confuse, frustrate and frighten him. It can break a pattern which the rapist is anticipating. Once this happens, you are buying time and significantly decreasing your chances of being raped.

An excellent way to distract someone is to simply do something they are not expecting. Ideally, this would be something that attracts others and forces him to lose control of the situation. Keep him guessing. Following are examples of how you can effectively distract your assailant.

Remember the questions involving you (hypothetically) being confronted by somebody in a confined area. Presumably, you have discerned that raping is on his mind. Compare your answers with what I am about to tell you.

Remembering that rapists dislike audiences, and considering that they hope you will tell no one about the attack, I came up with an idea in 1985 to help women when confronted by a rapist while in a confined area. My daughter who was venturing into babysitting at the time was the first recipient of this advice.

When confronted by an intruder who is lunging at you or if in the presence of an acquaintance whom you suspect has unwanted sexual advances on his mind, do the following:

- Immediately, put as much distance between you and the intruder, or acquaintance, as is possible.

- Pick up the first object that you can effectively hold in your hands. A book, bottle, vase, lamp, chair, etc. will suffice.

- Turn and throw the object through the first available window. If there is no window, throw the object through a television screen or against a wall. Break anything that you can get your hands on. As the old saying goes, "Create a ruckus."

- Look for an escape route.

- Visualize and plan a successful defense and escape.

- Breathe slowly and deeply to avoid panicking.

Most women who have answered questions 21 through 24 for me, have offered one of the following responses:

- Scream.

- No idea. Don't like to think about it. Hope it never happens.

- Confront him verbally.
- Kick him between the legs and attempt an escape.

Before elaborating upon my suggestion, let's look at the four other responses. First, they are exactly what most rapists will be anticipating and prepared to overcome.

- Screaming is fine except in most states, the windows are closed most of the year. Chances are, no one will hear you.

- If you have no idea of what to do now, you will probably have no idea of what to do during an actual attack. As mentioned earlier, you will most likely panic. Not liking to think about something only re-presses the thought - not the likelihood of it occurring. Hoping that something does not happen, although helpful to one's state of mind, falls short of absolute assurance. Hope needs an anchor that it can hold onto.

- Confronting a rapist verbally, either by yelling, criticizing, ridiculing or persuading may work. But, it is no simple task. As a young man ministering to incarcerated men and women behind bars, I soon learned how well they could size up an individual and decide how genuine he or she is. Many criminals are lacking in the usual forms of academic training, but their "street smart"

thinking is incredible. You can be read like a book. Remember too, that an acquaintance already knows something about you. Putting on an act of bravery may be the most difficult role playing in the world.

- Kicking a man between the legs is not always as easy as you think and he, again, will probably be expecting it.

I am not suggesting that these options are of no use. They can certainly help; almost anything can help. Doing nothing is what benefits the rapist most and leaves victims with the guilt of having failed to do anything to change the outcome of the attack. Executing a distraction technique can make a considerable difference.

- If you could break a window, your scream would have a realistic chance of being heard.

- Breaking the window, television screen, etc., is extreme and is probably something a rapist will not be expecting. He may very well think, "What the hell is she going to do next?" Another thought will most likely be, "Oh no, that broken window is going to be called into question by somebody, somewhere down the line." The important point here, particularly in date rape, is that he thinks this before he touches you. The attack is obviously not going down the way that he thought. The pattern is broken. His fear of an audience is immediately recalled. Since you are already attempting to attract attention and since some permanent damage (broken window, television, mirror, etc.) has taken place, his fear of you telling somebody is magnified. Who is panicking now? He is.

- Broken glass can be used as a weapon.

- If after the attack, you decide to go to court, you now have something going for you which some rape victims didn't have. Sometime during the trial, the broken glass or objects can be offered as circumstantial evidence to show and hopefully prove that you resisted. Everything broken or smashed will strongly suggest that you simply did not want the attack to take place.

Other distracting techniques that can be used in many situations include:

- Call out a man's name when being attacked. You may be able to fool the assailant into thinking someone is nearby.

- Scream "FIRE!" or "RAPE!" if you want to attract others.

- Mention someone's name you both know to create serious concern in the attacker's mind.

- Throw away your keys if attacked near your car door. Most public safety experts, martial artists, books, etc., would argue that you would be

throwing away an available weapon. Really? Don't you think that the average dirtbag in a parking lot attacking a woman has heard, read or seen this technique before? You have probably seen the technique before haven't you? Don't you think that when you bunch up the keys in your tightened fist, that maybe, just maybe, he will be looking for a strike toward his face? Place the keys in your fist sometime and lightly (I'm looking out for your well-being here) strike a hard surface with the tips of the keys a couple of times. Gradually and carefully increase the force of the blows. I'm sure that you will draw two conclusions from this experience. First, it is difficult to hold the keys in a stationary position. Second, it hurts. Another consideration for you to think about is whether this key strike will stop an attacker.

Well, if you ever decide to use your keys as a weapon, you better hope it works. Because if it doesn't, he has everything that he wants: you, the car and the keys. It should be noted that many women who are abducted (many of whom are raped), are abducted in their own vehicle. When you throw away the keys, his options are immediately diminished. At least, he cannot simply throw you in your vehicle and drive away with his victim.

• Scream continuously. Don't stop.

In chapter eight, you will notice how often I recommend using specific distraction techniques. Most battles with opponents are won in the psychological arena. Distractions are excellent tools to use.

DEFEND

Chapter four detailed some facts for you to ponder. I would like to remind you again that 71% of the women who physically resisted their attacker were not raped. I have heard all of the arguments against physically resisting. "Getting raped is better than dying!" "Fighting back just makes a rapist more angry and violent." That may be generally true. However, I have heard firsthand of rape victims who survived the attack, but were so abused, battered, and ravaged, that life, although still available, was no where near what it used to be.

The wife of a police officer shared with me the horrible sight which her husband witnessed while on patrol. A young girl had been attacked by two older youths. She had been repeatedly raped, beaten, tortured, passed on to other youths, again repeatedly raped, beaten and tortured.

Police officers who responded to the call were shocked at the sight of this little girl who was cut, bruised and bleeding on every part of her body. The woman's husband wept. Many emergency personnel at a nearby hospital could not hold back the tears. I am sure that the little girl's parent(s) wept with broken hearts. Yes, she survived and life was worth living, but I am sure that the little girl's life would be drastically altered. I am sure that police departments, emergency room personnel, rape crisis center counselors, and many others could describe similar tragedies in which women and children were raped and beaten.

What I am trying to say is that someone may threaten your life and have every intent to kill you if you don't cooperate. At that point, getting raped may be better than dying, but sometimes - barely better. Since you don't know what will happen to you above and beyond the rape, even if you are cooperative, then you ought to give yourself a fighting chance. It may very well be your only chance to survive the attack.

Whether a rapist attacking you is a cold-blooded killer can be difficult to decide. Ted Bundy traveled the country not only as a rapist but a plotting, manipulative, and masqueraded murderer. In Michigan, Leslie Williams, a man recently convicted for murder and rape in Michigan, attacked several women, killing some and apparently deciding to allow others to live. Each victim had no idea if they would survive the attack or not. Therefore, my advise for you is to put up the fight of your life for your life. Do whatever it takes to overcome. Punch, gouge, kick, tear, push, elbow, knee, twist, scratch, bite. Do whatever you must to survive.

Every living, breathing and thinking creature on this earth has some kind of survival instinct. There is a fighting side in all of us. You need only to learn when and how to activate this survival instinct. It's amazing to me how boaters and swimmers have survived shark attacks by simply kicking, punching and yelling. Apparently, a clear message of strong resistance prevailed. Remember, statistics on rape support my position.

Concerning the argument that resisting will only enrage a rapist, almost all researchers agree that, among other emotions, a rapist is "angry" to begin with. Don't worry about getting him mad; he already is. Don't worry about being discourteous in your attempt to avoid physical injury. He will probably physically injure you in one way or another anyway.

Moreover, if you fear worsening the pain or injury by resisting, victims of forced vaginal and anal penetration will tell you that the pain endured from those acts were as painful as any other injury. Remember:

- Your primary concern is to minimize injury to yourself.

- Maintain an appropriate respect for an offender. Don't overestimate his capabilities, but, above all else, don't underestimate your own.

- Remember you are the innocent one. Defend yourself and strike out at the offender with an attitude of righteous indignation.

In the next chapter, take a close look at the self-defense techniques. Read the instructions carefully and practice them. They are there for you and every other woman like you. If you believe anything which I have written, believe this - those techniques can offer you protection. I have handpicked them, tested them and wholeheartedly recommend them.

DEPART

I observed several self--defense "experts" who were invited to speak on the Oprah Winfrey show. A man was dressed up in a heavily padded outfit which reminded me of the cartoon character used in the Michelin Tire commercials. Women from the audience were invited to strike out at this slow-moving, Frankenstein character. The participants were shown some self-defense techniques to attempt. Apparently, the first required technique was to fall to the ground in a curled up position. The thinking behind this technique suggested that a woman does not have adequate strength and balance when standing to effectively execute an offensive technique. To my amazement, the studio audience seemed to agree.

Several women were approached by this padded giant. Each one fell to the ground, curled up into a fetal position, and waited for the attacker to slowly walk toward them. Once the attacker was within striking distance, a kick was delivered toward the assailant's groin or knees. Each time, the padded attacker fell to the ground. Without exception, the participants continued striking as the audience cheered. The padded attacker was struck several times before the woman decided to leave.

Overall, I thought the program was informative; but, the simulated attacks were simply not true to life. The techniques fooled a studio and viewing audience, but they would never in a million years fool a rapist. They limited the options available to a potential victim. A kick to the knee does not require extensive training, balance nor strength. An individual does not need to fall to the ground to properly execute such a technique.

I'll tell you what dropping to the ground does. It significantly decreases your chances of escaping and drastically increases your chances of being raped since a rapist often wants you positioned there anyway. Also, a man who sees the woman he is

attacking fall to the ground, and cock up one leg close to her chest is likely going to see what is on her mind. He will clearly see her telegraphing what she is about to do. He also will not walk at her in the same slow-motion and unsuspecting fashion as did this padded giant. It just won't happen.

I've already stated as well that I am not a strong believer in training you to go to the second round in a confrontation. True, the first technique could cause the attacker to fall. But don't press your luck. He will not make the same mistake twice.

Continuing to follow-up with less devastating techniques offers him a chance to subdue you and take revenge. If one technique frees you from an assailant, get out of there immediately. If one technique does not work, follow up with additional strikes, but only to enable you to immediately escape. When he is momentarily incapacitated, it is time to exit. Get out of there.

My position is that your primary goal should be to avoid getting hurt in your attempt to escape. The goal should not be to concentrate on how much damage you can inflict. Think about it. I wish I could have had five minutes on her show to voice what is now being written.

The five D's complete the rape prevention system. Memorize them. Think about them. Expand upon them. But most importantly, place some trust and confidence in them. In the next chapter, you will be introduced to several stretching and self-defense techniques which I believe are ideally suited for women. At first, these techniques should be practiced in slow-motion and, as with any new physical endeavor, with permission or approval from a physician. Gradually increase the speed and force of the techniques as your flexibility and coordination improve.

No one has the right to rape you. In your mine, this needs to be more than a preference; it needs to be a conviction - one supported by determination and preparation. One way to strengthen this conviction, is to strengthen your defense. Psychological techniques were presented in the last chapter, and perhaps you thought, "Yeah, but what if that doesn't work? What if he keeps attacking? Then what?" Then you have no other choice but to physically defend yourself. The following techniques are designed for that purpose.

Note: As with any form of exercise or strenuous activity, you should consult your doctor before engaging in the following activities. All techniques should be practiced slowly until the mechanics of each are learned and sufficient flexibility is attained.

STRETCHING EXERCISES

Most martial artists and athletes recognize the importance of proper stretching before actively participating in physically demanding exercises. Proper stretching enables you to:

• Warm up the body

• Develop flexibility

• Increase blood circulation

• Relax and concentrate on self-defense techniques

• Avoid injuries

My rules of thumb, when it comes to stretching are:

• Stretch slowly and smoothly without any quick or bobbing movements.

• Do not overextend or stretch to the point where you are experiencing pain or muscle tightness which are too uncomfortable to endure.

• Dedicate enough time (at least 10 minutes) to adequately prepare the body for practice. The muscles will be stretched and the body will be "warmed up" for more strenuous activity.

• Since self-defense techniques usually require using different parts of the body, a complete body stretch is highly recommended. Start at the neck and work your way down your body.

• Remember to breathe slowly and deeply.

Neck

Stand straight with your legs approximately 18 inches apart. Place your hands on your hips and slowly begin to rotate your head in clockwise fashion. Extend in each direction as far as you can with a reasonable feeling of comfort. Make approximately 10 rotations and then reverse the direction. See Figure 7-1.

Next, look straight ahead with your chin up. Slowly look back over you right shoulder. Try to keep your torso facing

Figure 7-1

directly in front of you. Hold your head in that position for 10 seconds and then repeat this movement looking over your left shoulder. See Figure 7-2.

Figure 7-2

While in the same stance, drop your head forward and slowly attempt to touch your chin on your chest. Hold for ten seconds.

Next, tilt your head directly backward and look behind you as far as possible. Hold for ten seconds. Incidentally, as you will see later, these movements will help you in executing head strikes and looking over your shoulder quickly.

Arms And Shoulders

Standing in the same position with your feet approximately 18 inches apart, straighten your arms and tighten your hands into a fist. Slowly begin rotating your arms forward in a circular motion. Try to make the circle as wide as possible. Make ten full rotations and then reverse the direction. Begin with wide circles and gradually reduce the size while increasing speed. See Figures 7-3 and 7-4.

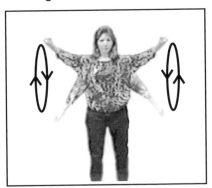

Figure 7-3

Figure 7-4

Wrists

Straighten the fingers on one hand while tucking the thumb in close. Slowly force the fingers backward with the other hand. Hold for ten seconds. Repeat on the other hand.

Stretch the fingers in the other direction by putting pressure on the top of the hand. Hold for ten seconds on each hand.

Figure 7-5

Torso/Waist

Standing in the same position, place your closed fists next to your sternum with each elbow lifted up in a parallel position. Look over your right shoulder and rotate the upper body in the same direction. Attempt to extend the elbow as if attempting to strike something. (Some day, you might be required to.) Once you have fully extended the elbow in that direction, look over the opposite shoulder and rotate the upper body in that direction. Again, completely extend the elbow accordingly. Be sure to keep your feet planted firmly on the ground while performing this exercise. Vary the height of the simulated elbow strikes. See Figures 7-5 and 7-6.

Another good exercise for the torso and waist is to widen your stance with your hands placed on your hips. Bend the knees slightly. Slowly lean forward. Begin to rotate the body in a clockwise direction. Complete 10 rotations and then reverse the direction.

Figure 7-6

Legs/Knees

Stand with your legs straightened and approximately 18 inches apart. Slowly lean forward and extend your arms toward the floor as far as you can without bending your knees or overextending. Once you have reached your maximum stretch, hold for 10 seconds. See Figure 7-7.

Figure 7-7

Figure 7-8

Figure 7-9

Stand next to a chair, counter, table, etc., Keep both legs straight. Lift one leg up on the object. Slowly reach for your toes and stretch them back toward you. Be sure to keep the lifted leg as straight as possible. Slowly lean forward toward your foot and hold for ten seconds. Repeat the stretch on the other leg. Raise the leg to a height which can be comfortably maintained. Do not overextend. See Figure 7-8.

Do the same movement, except this time rotate the leg so that the foot is not facing upward but to the side. The foot which you are standing on should be turned in the same direction as well. Perform the stretch on each side for ten seconds. See Figure 7-9.

Sit on the floor with both feet extended and spread apart as far as is comfortable. Slowly lean toward each foot and straight ahead for twenty seconds. Be sure to keep both legs straight, and if possible, grab your toes and stretch them back toward you. Try to relax while performing these movements. See Figure 7-10.

Figure 7-10

Remember to breathe slowly and deeply.

Sit down and draw each heel as close as you can into the groin area. Slowly press down on each knee for a few seconds in an attempt to touch the knee to the floor. Pressing downward with your elbows will further enhance this stretch. See Figures 7-11 and 7-12.

Figure 7-11

Figure 7-12

Next, extend one leg up in front of you and attempt to hold the heel while straightening the leg. Hold for ten seconds. Repeat the stretch on the other leg. See Figure 7-13.

Lie on your back and pull up one knee close to the chest. Hold it close to the body with your arms. Hold the stretch on

Figure 7-13

each side for ten seconds. See Figure 7-14.

Figure 7-14

Sit next to a wall with your back touching its surface. While staying close to the wall, roll over on your back while extending your legs. Make sure that the backs of your legs are resting against the wall. Slowly spread your legs until comfortably stretched. Hold for one full minute. At the conclusion of the stretch, use your hands to help lift the stretched out legs. This is an excellent technique effectively stretch the legs. See Figure 7-15.

Figure 7-15

Figure 7-17

Stretch Kicks

Front

Stand next to a wall with one foot behind the other. While holding unto the wall, straighten the leg next to the wall and lift it straight up in front of you making sure that you do not overextend. Perform 10 repetitions on each side.

Do five stretches with the toes pointed up and pulled back. Do five with the foot extended and the toes pointed away. See Figures 7-16 and 7-17.

Do not overextend. Perform 10 repetitions on each leg. Alternate the foot positions as above.

Note: The front and back stretch kicks can be performed together. These stretching exercises do not take much time to perform and can greatly affect your ability to do other techniques. Refer to Figures 7-16 & 7-17.

Side

Stand facing a wall with your feet spread apart slightly. Straighten your legs and lift one leg up directly to the side. Do not overextend. Perform 10 repetitions on each side. Again, alternate toes up and toes extended.

General/Warm-up

Running in place, sit-ups, jumping jacks, jogging, jumping rope, aerobics, etc. can be performed with your self-defense training either as warmup or as follow-up exercises. I strongly recommend that you practice running in place after you stretch for about one minute.

Figure 7-16

Back

While facing the wall, lean forward, straighten one leg. Lift the leg up behind you while looking at it over the shoulder.

Another excellent warm-up exercise is to stand erect and raise each knee toward your chest. It is a good idea to alternate lifting the knees vertically and diagonally. I usually have students place their palms face down at waist level. Attempt to strike the palms of your hands as you raise the knees. Since lifting the knee when executing a kick is extremely important, this one minute exercise can prove to be an important part of your training.

Additionally, for best results, perform sit-ups by bending the knees and lifting the head & upper torso slightly. See Figure 7-18.

Figure 7-18

RAPE PREVENTION TECHNIQUES

Remember what I said earlier about making a would-be rapist pay. If he plans to rape you, then you make sure, by executing one or more of the following techniques, that it will cost him something. I would not present the following techniques if I did not believe you could execute them effectively. I have been in do-or-die situations, and one thing always comes to mind; anything that I do is usu-ally better than doing nothing at all. Baseball players, female and male, young and old, always seem just a little less frustrated after making an out on a third swinging strike than when taking a called third strike, knowing they did absolutely nothing.

Physical techniques are indeed your final defense. This is what you do when all else fails. I've been told that armies have proven most powerful when they had no other option than to fight. They had nowhere to escape and no way out. It was do or die. Read carefully the following information on self-defense techniques. Try them and practice them. If ever attacked, they will probably surprise both you and your attacker concerning their effectiveness. These are the tricks you pull out of your bag as a last resort. Remember that a rapist is also most vulnerable to an attack when he least expects it. The following techniques will surprise, hurt, immobilize and frustrate him. Most rapists will be telling you, "Trust me, do what I say and you won't be hurt." I'm suggesting that you trust me and invest some time in learning and practicing the following techniques.

I don't believe in luck. I believe that proper preparation and determination, coupled with enough courage to keep yourself from quitting, will do more for you than all the "luck" in the world.

Chapter Seven - RAPE PREVENTION TECHNIQUES

"For all your days prepare, and meet them all alike: When you are the anvil, bear. When you are the hammer, strike."
- Edwin Markham

Proper Distancing

Before discussing fighting stances, or blocking, kicking or punching techniques, I would like to introduce you to the most important and effective technique ever taught to me. This technique fits in with my martial arts philosophy which emphasizes not maximizing what injury you inflict on another, but rather controlling and limiting what injury is inflicted upon you. In a threatening confrontation with an assailant, you need time to react and to prepare a strong defense. Although some surprise attacks will prohibit having ample time, many attacks involve an initial contact with an assailant from a distance of about two feet or more. Unfortunately, most Americans, particularly men, have been conditioned to "get in somebody's face" before things escalate into a physical struggle. Most of us are content to use our mouths before using our fists. The danger of getting nose to nose with a threatening individual is that you are vulnerable to a surprise assault or what is commonly called a "sucker punch." In such instances, your opponent has picked the exact moment of his attack and has not allowed you to make adequate preparation.

In his book, Signals, Allan Please describes what he calls "social zones" and "intimate zones." He examines how the distance between ourselves and others affects our social behavior. Please considers a "social zone" to be between four feet and twelve feet. An "intimate zone" is much closer at six to eighteen inches (Please, 1984, p. 26). Everyone has their own definition of "their space." When defending against a rapist or when in the presence of someone you simply suspect may have raping you on his mind, six to eighteen inches is more than intimate; it is dangerous.

As a teenager, I followed the Vietnam War closely after a good friend of mine was killed over there. The military term "demilitarized zone" (DMZ) was often mentioned.

That area was supposedly a buffer zone, a restricted area that was no-man's land, separating the opposing armies. One thing was certain, this was a highly volatile and dangerous area to be in. It was not really secured by anybody; it was just there.

What could happen in this defined space was anybody's guess and everybody's fear. I often refer to military terms such as the DMZ when teaching rape-prevention since a confrontation with a rapist has all of the elements of warfare. In fact, rape is always a part of war. Susan Brownmiller expounds upon this. "When men are men, slugging it out among themselves, conquering new land, subjugating new people, driving on toward victory, unquestionably there shall be some raping." Historically in warfare, women in conquered lands have been viewed as a soldier's "lawful booty" (Brownmiller, 1975, pp. 31, 70).

How does the term DMZ apply to you when defending against rape? It is the term I use to describe the space just beyond arms reach, between you and an assailant. See Figure 7-19.

Figure 7-19

A man who is within reaching distance of you is inside the DMZ, and once this close, places you in a precarious position. The DMZ is where bodily injury is inflicted and where assailants do the most harm. The principle was taught to me twenty years ago, and looking back, it has proven to be an important lesson. By properly distancing myself from threatening individuals, I never gave them the edge which they were accustomed to having. Sucker punching me was impossible because the assailant had to commit himself by covering the distance between us. Covering the distance, even if suddenly lunging, took time to do. That precious time gave me time to react; time to defend; time to pull out my own little bag of tricks.

Over the years, I have somewhat perfected this technique so that when forced to back away in a threatening situation, I do so casually and tactfully. My goal is always to back away just beyond arm's length.

Creating a distance between you and the threatening individual:

- Allows you to converse with him from a safe distance

- Forces the individual to step forward to make any type of contact with you

- Offers you ample time to react to the attack

- Significantly increases your chances of escape

- Communicates a strong message of awareness - "I don't have a problem talking to you, but if you are who you say you are, talk to me from there."

- Increases the number of self-defense techniques which can be used

Once an aggressor enters the DMZ, my recommendation is that as you back away, attempt to turn slightly sideways if possible.

Turning part of your side to an opponent limits the vulnerable areas on your body which he can injure. It also increases your balance if you are attacked and allows you to execute more powerful techniques. See Figure 7-20.

Figure 7-20

Evasive Techniques

If you can avoid a conflict entirely by running away, consider the famous Nike commercial message: DO IT!. Run! If you can effectively defend against a rapist by momentarily retreating and then counterattacking, DO IT! The problem is that avoiding physical contact is not an easy task. Therefore, I have included two techniques which have served me well over the years.

Head Fade

Larry Malo, my first martial arts instructor, mastered this technique and taught it to thousands. After turning sideways toward an opponent, he would simply stand there with his hands at his sides. As the opponent would attempt to strike out at him, Larry would simply hold his ground and tilt the upper body away from the attacking fist or object. See Figure 7-21.

Figure 7-21

Remarkably, he developed several ways of combining this evasive technique with offensive strikes. For example, sometimes he would perform the head fade and when recovering, he would thrust a back fist strike, or he would execute the back fist strike and then use the head fade. Simultaneously striking and performing the head fade works best for me. See Figure 7-22.

Figure 7-22

Side-Stepping

Tom Smith, who owns and operates Shaolin Kung-Fu in Westland, Michigan teaches a martial art which places a strong emphasis on sidestepping an attack and then immediately counterattacking. I enrolled my children and myself in his school after watching his smooth and lightning fast sidestepping techniques. At least 75% of the self-defense techniques Tom teaches are combined with a sidestepping action which precedes the counterattack. This technique is done by quickly shuffling to the right or left of the incoming attack. Tom suggests that the foot nearest the direction to which you are stepping should move first with the other foot following. Counter-attacks can be delivered as you sidestep or immediately afterward.

Note: I recommend side-stepping if the situation so allows. Darting off to one side helps deflect the blow and confuse the assailant.

It also creates an opportunity to effectively counter-attack from an angle which the assailant is least likely to expect. If sidestepping is not possible due to a lack of time or space, the head fade can be used.

Cross-over Stepping

Crossing one foot over the other can sometimes give you a tremendous advantage by offering leverage to a technique and exposing a vulnerable area of an opponent. See Figure 7-23.

Figure 7-23

For example, if an assailant "bear hugs" you from behind, cross one foot over the other, thereby opening his groin, and then deliver a hammer fist strike to the groin, followed with a head strike to the face. Ouch! See Figure 7-24.

Figure 7-24

Proper Breathing

The way you breathe can have quite an impact on how your body functions. Ask any woman who did the Lamaze breathing technique while giving birth. Watch competitive weight-lifters before they pick up the bar. They breathe deeply and psyche up for the lift. Breathing is controlled for optimal physical control. On the contrary, people who are suddenly frightened tend to lose control of their breathing. They either hold their breath or they begin to breathe rapidly and uncontrollably.

In threatening situations, you must make a concerted effort to maintain control of your breathing. Losing control of your breathing can cause light-headedness and weakness. You have probably heard someone remark that they had their wind knocked out of them. If frightened enough, it seems you can have your wind scared out of you. I'll never forget the time that my brother Terry, a neighbor David Harry, and I were sitting on a curb down the street from where we lived. It was around 10:00 in the evening and we were sitting there talking and joking to kill time. Suddenly, in the silence of the evening, someone behind us screamed in the most horrifying manner imaginable. We knew instantly by the voice that this was not one of our friends pulling a prank. This was a crazy scream from an apparently crazy person. It was at that point that I learned how some things can defy gravity and the laws of physics. I know that to be true, because when we heard that scream, we were instantly air-born and seemingly moving faster than our bodies were humanly capable. After running at what seemed to be Olympic qualifying speeds, we arrived at David's house. The run didn't wind us, the scream did. We were breathing hard for a long time afterward due to fright.

I can't remember who taught me this breathing technique for fighting, but it has always helped me to control my breathing. When out of breath, I slowly inhale through the nose and exhale with two short breaths through the mouth. A concerted effort should be made to breathe from the diaphragm as opposed to breathing more in the chest. Repeat this technique two or three times. If this doesn't seem to work, simply try to breathe more deeply and slowly.

I have another tale to tell but an important principle comes along with it. I remember every moment of it in detail as if it happened yesterday.

I was a sophomore in high school which means I was somewhere between 16 and 17 years old. I walked out of a high school dance with Dave Dismuke, a high school friend. As we reached my red, 1962 Corvair, a black, 1966 Pontiac GTO convertible pulled up with several guys quickly piling out. They looked about four years older and a foot taller. I didn't like the odds and definitely didn't like having to be there. The group approached Dave and one of them punched him in his mouth before he could use it. By that time I was sitting in the driver's seat hoping that they would disappear or that I would. The group circled my side of the car and some goon twice my size used a few expletives in telling me to get out. After weighing the pros and cons for one -one-thousandth of a second, I got out of the car. The goon didn't waste any words in telling me that if I didn't have any money, I would no

longer have any teeth. He quickly convinced me that I would look worse than Dave. I didn't feel like debating, and apparently neither did he. I had little martial arts training but had learned that controlling my breathing was a necessity. I remember breathing deeply and hearing the nervousness in my voice. I reached down in my pocket and felt a few dollars and several quarters. The money was tips I had earned delivering pizzas. I don't know why I took all of the money out of the pocket, but perhaps I thought it would buy me a reprieve. I paused for a moment and breathed deeply again. My thoughts and actions in the next twenty seconds surprised me. It bothered me that this guy was going to get my tip money and, probably with or without the help of his cronies, clean my clock. I then did something which was really out of character for me. I breathed deeply, took out all the money in one hand, reached down and picked up one quarter. I breathed deeply and slowly as I put the money back in my pocket and handed him the quarter. He stood there in disbelief for what seemed like forever. He took the quarter with a shocked look on his face, looked over each shoulder at his cohorts, shrugged and walked away. No one said a word. He had one quarter and I still had my teeth.

I've often wondered about that ordeal. You would grow old

trying to convince me that controlling my breathing didn't help. I controlled the pace of things and I did something else which helps in such situations. I didn't look angry and I didn't look afraid. That is bewildering to someone attempting to threaten and control you. I was nervous but apparently it didn't show.

Over the years, I have attempted to perfect the breathing technique and have tried to teach it to others. In threatening situations, concentrate on breathing slowly and deeply. While you are breathing deeply, concentrate on how you can immediately distract and defend. Assess your options. Depending on the situation, it might be difficult to breathe quietly and slowly. If so, then attempt to inhale deeply through your nostrils and exhale strongly through your mouth. This is exactly what you may have seen professional boxers and competitive swimmers do prior to engaging in their sports.

Concentrating on your breathing can help you in preparing for physical activity. Offensively, breathing plays a different role. Be sure that whenever you execute a technique that you exhale. Holding the breath impedes fluidity and speed of movement.

Fighting Stances

Having studied several martial arts, I have used several stances in sparring and fighting situations and others for noncom-

batant patterns and forms. Each stance has its advantages and disadvantages depending on the situation. Two years ago, I wrote a general physical assault awareness and prevention program for a training company in Troy, Michigan. It was presented to UAW-Ford and UAW-Chrysler employees. Because the program was designed mostly for men in their mid- to late-forties, and because the focus was not rape prevention, rather it was an introduction to practical self-defense, the stances I chose were better suited for men. The UAW training centers were not interested in any program which had a strong emphasis on traditional martial arts. Fortunately, in this book, I have the liberty to focus on two stances which are ideally suited for women, particularly when it comes to rape prevention.

There are strong arguments for and against a woman positioning herself in a karate-type stance when attacked. Some would argue that if a woman faces somebody in a karate stance, she is telegraphing her intentions and forewarning her assailant of her training. Others recommend a relaxed, normal stance from which certain techniques can still be executed with the element of surprise. Frankly, I recommend both. The situation will usually dictate which stance is most appropriate. All self-defense techniques presented in this chapter can be executed using either stance.

Casual Fighting Stance

This stance is deceptively effective. The positions of the hands and feet do not necessarily telegraph your intentions and yet your body is positioned to execute further self-defense techniques. The stance involves turning your side slightly toward the assailant. Your feet should be approximately 18 inches or shoulder width apart. Hands should be at your sides.

All of the techniques to which you will be introduced can easily be done from this relaxed and protective position. Most likely, your casual stance will not be perceived as a fighting posture. It should also be mentioned that a surprise attack could limit your reaction time, and therefore make the casual stance your only option. Always remember that the element of surprise is still in your corner. By the time he realizes what you are doing, it will be too late for him to react. Figure 7-25 illustrates one practical and yet deceptive way to position yourself in the casual fighting stance.

Figure 7-25

Formal Fighting Stance

In 1976, I studied Aikido in Detroit while finishing my senior year in college. I was instructed to position myself in a stance which instantly reminded me of a samurai's body positioning while holding a sword. I cannot remember if it was the instructor or another student, but someone commented that students must learn to trust the stance. It reminded me of what was taught to me back in 1972 while training in a full-contact karate school. Larry Malo, the owner of the school, instructed students to position themselves in a protective stance, tighten the fists, and psyche up for battle. It worked. There were times when, as a beginning student, I was matched with an opponent who, at that time, had superior martial arts skills. Nevertheless, I was trained to move into a fighting stance, trust it and mentally prepare myself for whatever might lie ahead. In a full-contact training format, you had to trust something.

Having trained in six different martial arts, and observed others, I have had many opportunities to compare styles. Although some may emphasize snapping punches as opposed to rigid, full-extension techniques; and low kicks as opposed to high, etc., many fundamentals of the techniques are quite similar. The various martial arts around the world are more alike than they are different. This holds true for fighting stances as well. There are some styles which use unique fighting stances, but generally, most are quite similar. Most martial arts recommend turning the body slightly sideways to protect the vital areas of the body, bending the knees, positioning the feet shoulder width apart and holding the arms close to the body for protection. This is my recommendation as well. Such a stance is illustrated in Figure 7-26.

In certain circumstances I like a formal fighting stance which offers optimal protection without restricting any necessary body movement. In other words, I prefer to position my-

self so that I can quickly and easily execute both defensive and offensive movements. I even like the fact that if no movement was initiated, the body is still somewhat protected. A formal stance can also be intimidating.

Figure 7-26

Some important points to be remembered about a formal fighting stance are:

- Turn your side slightly toward your opponent.

- Position your feet shoulder width apart with one foot behind and slightly off to the side.

- Bend the knees slightly.

- Place the hands in loosely clenched fists close to the body. The back hand should be under the chin. The other hand should be in front of the body - partially extended with the fist about solar plexus high.

I honestly cannot recommend this fighting stance over a relaxed but deceptively prepared stance. Both have proven effective for me in the past. However, you should be aware that once you have thrown a kick or hand technique, the cat is out of the bag. Your attacker will be on to the fact that you have had some type of training. You may as well move into the formal fighting stance, trust it, and be ready to go.

NOTE: Trusting your fighting stance will help you to trust other techniques.

Of course, the situation could arise whereby you decide to position yourself in the formal fighting position, execute a technique, and then if unable to escape, reposition yourself into

a casual fighting stance as if giving up. Of course, you won't be. Too bad for him that he doesn't know that. There are still several tricks which can be played such as fakes, setup techniques, hand and foot combinations, etc.

Incidentally, I don't recommend watching his eyes since this can be distracting. It is his hands and body which will inflict injury. Look at the middle of his chest. This enables you to see the whole picture.

Fighting Stance - Prone Position

The situation could arise where you are knocked to the ground or are lying down when confronted by a rapist. I recommend that you position your hands to support your upper body and that you draw your legs and feet close in toward the torso. You will look as if you are coiling up for protection, but you will have your leg positioned to kick. Make sure that you are braced to kick hard and positioned to get to your feet as quickly as possible.

Remember though, lying on your back or side severely limits the techniques you can use. Worse, it offers the rapist more control and increases the odds of you being raped. Think about it; he already has you where he wants you. See Figures 7-27 & 7-28.

Figure 7-27

Figure 7-28

Foot/knee Techniques

Side Kick

I chose this as the first striking technique to introduce since it is extremely effective, relatively easy to learn, does not require much speed or power and is most deceptive. Although commonly called a sidekick, I have limited its application to the knees.

As you become more flexible, improve your balance, and develop this kick, it can then be applied higher on an assailant's body, preferably the rib area. It is one rape prevention technique which you must discipline yourself to practice. The technique will not let you down.

Remember the limping football player.

The kick is executed by first lifting the knee of the kicking leg toward the chest while drawing the foot close to the body. The foot should be positioned so that the heel and outside edge of the foot are extended. This can be accomplished by curling the toes up and pointing the foot inward. The leg which you are standing on should be slightly bent with the heel angled toward the attacker. The arms should be held close to the body.

Once the foot is cocked close to the body, the kick is performed by thrusting the foot out toward your target. The leg should be extended about 95% to avoid overextending and risking knee injury. Once contact is made, the leg should be retracted close to the body for protection, balance and possibly another technique. The kick should be directed at the knee. If you miss the knee, a kick delivered just below or above the knee will still inflict injury. The following picture illustrates how to execute the entire movement. Remember, if you are not kicking at a training pad or bag, do not kick full speed. See Figure 7-29.

Back Kick

Since none of us have eyes in the backs of our heads, it is understandable why attacks are often directed toward this area. Rapists have most of the cards

Lift Knee Up High

Figure 7-29

in their favor when attacking you from behind, except one. They risk being kicked when reaching for you.

The back kick is one of the most powerful martial arts techniques in the world. It will probably catch an attacker by surprise and it will catch him with a thrusted heel which will feel as if he was kicked by a horse. A back kick delivered toward the knee for example is devastating.

The technique is also most useful when attempting to escape. If you are attempting to run away and in spite of your efforts, notice that someone is about to grab you, quickly stopping and using this technique is not difficult. If someone is chasing you up stairs, a back kick which would normally strike somebody in the knees would be head level.

Remember, you can always act as if you are beginning to run, stop, and then thrust the heel toward your reaching assailant. Also, the kick can be thrown with either foot, regardless which foot is closest to your opponent.

To execute the back kick, simply lift up the knee toward the chest, draw the foot in close behind, and position the foot so that the heel is fully extended. The foot position is achieved by lifting the toes up and in toward the other leg. Hold the position firmly. Lean forward and thrust the foot toward your target with 95% extension. Once contact is made, retract the foot to its previous position.

Let me just say this. If you hit him anywhere with this technique, it is going to hurt. If you can focus this kick to the knees, groin or ribs, he will no longer be the threat that he once was. That's a fact.

Note: This kick with its foot position can be used to stomp the top of an assailant's foot.

Figure 7-30 illustrates how to properly position the foot and execute the technique.

Front Kick (Forward Thrust)

This is a quick and relatively easy kick to learn. To execute the kick, simply raise the knee slightly higher than the plane on which you plan to focus the kick. Position your foot close to the body to ensure a full kick and point the foot upward with the toes curled up. The striking portion of the foot is what is

Lift Knee Up High

Figure 7-30

Front Kick (Upward Thrust)

The mechanics for this technique closely resemble those of the above mentioned kick except the foot position and the focus. For this kick, the toes and the top part of the foot are pointed down and forward. The striking portion can range from the shin to the top of the foot.

commonly called the ball of the foot. Quickly thrust the foot out to approximately 95% extension.

Once contact is made, quickly retract the foot to its previous position. This kick incorporates more of a snapping motion. The groin and stomach are primary targets for beginners. Either the front or back leg can be used for the technique. Figure 7-31 illustrates the mechanics of this technique.

The focus of the kick should be about one foot past the targeted area. When the groin is the primary target, the kick should be focused half way up his torso to ensure that you will have maximum speed and thrust when making contact with the groin.

Reach for the sky. Lift that leg as high as you possibly can and his voice will do the same thing. Raping you will lose its place on his priority list.

The mechanics of this technique are shown in Figure 7-32. If ever attacked up close, focus your kick between his legs and let it fly.

Knee Kick

The knee strike is much slower than the above mentioned techniques, but few techniques rival it for power. The following pictures best describe this technique. Simply lift the knee quickly and thrust it into your target. The knee can be thrust upward or diagonally. It is helpful to grab the back of an attacker's head or shoulder when delivering the kick. See Figures 7-33 & 7-34.

Figure 7-31

Lift Knee
Swing Foot in Arc

Figure 7-32

Figure 7-33

Hand Techniques

The techniques I have chosen work well even if hands are not large or particularly strong. Guess whose hands fit that description? Even long nails will not interfere. Women I have trained may not have had the strength and power of most men, but they did have good hand speed and coordination.

Figure 7-34

Back Knuckle Strike

This is my personal favorite. The back knuckle strike is simple to learn and probably has more applications for street use than any other technique. The strike is not as powerful, penetrating or forceful as some other hand techniques, but in self-defense situations, it is most effective due to its versatility and speed. Martial artists usually practice strong, rigid punches when performing patterns (forms/katas) or breaking bricks and boards, but when it comes to sparring (fighting practice), they quite often revert to this technique.

The back knuckle strike is extremely quick, can be delivered from almost every angle and if delivered to the head or ribs, it will stun an opponent. The strike also works well in combination with other hand and foot techniques.

The back knuckle strike is delivered by slightly raising the elbow toward the target with your hand remaining close to the body; then, quickly thrust or snap your fist toward the target. As you are doing this, your wrist should be bent. As your fist nears the target, begin to flex the wrist to roll the knuckles over as you tighten the fist. The striking portion of the hand is the index and middle knuckles. The mechanics are similar to the motion involved with snapping a wet towel. An important step to remember is that as you near the target, continually tighten the fist. This will significantly increase the hand speed. The trajectory of the strike is unlimited. Once contact is made, immediately retract the hand to its original position. The technique should be delivered in a snapping motion. The target areas for this technique are almost unlimited. See Figure 7-35.

Hammer-Fist Strike

This technique does not require much explanation. Simply close your fingers into a loosely clenched fist as you draw the hand toward the body. Using the elbow as a hinge, push the edge of the hand toward the target, tightening the fist as you near it. The hammer-fist strike can be delivered effectively from almost any angle. Although the technique is relatively easy to throw, its effectiveness and

power are surprising. The technique can be delivered into the throat, face, ribs, groin or back of the neck. Again, after contact is made, quickly retract the hand. See Figure 7-36.

Figure 7-35

Figure 7-36

Palm Strike

This is a devastating, powerful technique particularly when in close. To do the technique, put your hand in front of you with the fingers and thumb close together and pointing upward. Tilt your fingers as far back as they will go. Your hand should be tilted back to the point where you could set a cup on your palm. Tuck the thumb in close. Bend the finger tips slightly forward. Draw the hand close to the body, preferably near the waist. The palm should face the target. Thrust the hand toward the target with a 95% extension of the arm. The striking surface is the bottom portion of the palm. The hand should be tensed when striking. Once contact is made, quickly retract the hand back to its original position. The target areas are the chin, nose and solar plexus. If you invert the hand position (palm up), the palm strike can be used as a groin technique. The strike also serves as an excellent technique to push somebody away from you when attempting to create some distance between you and your attacker. Observe Figures 7-37 & 7-38 to better understand the mechanics and applications of this technique.

Figure 7-37

Figure 7-38

Chapter Seven - RAPE PREVENTION TECHNIQUES

Y-Hand Strike

This technique is performed by placing the four fingers close together and bending them slightly. Spread the thumb and fingers apart. Tilt the hand so the Y-shaped portion of the hand is centered. Although the fingers are slightly bent, they should be tensed. With the hand positioned palm down and near your waist, thrust the webbed portion of the hand toward the attacker's throat. Deliver this technique in a snapping motion. After contact, immediately retract the hand back to its former position. Like the palm strike, the Y-hand technique works well in "close encounters" of the worst kind. See Figure 7-39.

Figure 7-39

Thumb/Finger Strikes

I believe most women would use their nails to scratch an assailant before using them for anything else. It makes sense. Scratching doesn't take any special training and can inflict injury. Unfortunately, I don't think scratching a man's skin will get the job done. Using fingers and nails for poking at the eyes and jabbing at the throat could be more effective. For example, if a man facing you suddenly "bear hugs" you, it's easy to place your fingers on each side of his temple and thrust your thumb nails into the eyes. Sound gruesome? It is, but it will be easier to deal with his injury than with what he might do to you. See Figure 7-40.

Figure 7-40

Jabbing the thumbs into the front of the throat can be a man stopper as well. Place your thumbs into the tender portion of your own throat to appreciate what I am recommending. Jabbing the eyes with the end of your fingers can be easier than trying to scratch at them. You can attempt to do both however. Also, use your fingers to grab a handful of his hair. Pulling his hair can control the movement of his head and upper body.

Elbow Techniques

When in close with someone attempting to rape you, the elbows if used properly, can put anybody down. I mean anybody. I don't care if you are 103 pounds and have been fasting for two weeks, using your elbows with some control will stun and injure a man trying to hurt you. Although elbow strikes are usually slower than hand techniques, that bony elbow comes across like a ball peen hammer when connecting.

Robert Brown, a good friend of mine and a superb martial artist, comes to mind when I think of elbow strikes. I think he executes these techniques as well as anyone else I've met. At a whopping 135 pounds soaking wet, this guy compensates for his lack of size with dazzling elbow techniques. I asked him how he developed the techniques. His response was that he did not concentrate on power, but on speed.

There is enough muscle behind the technique from the arms, chest and shoulders. The key is to swing that elbow as quickly as you can and to focus past the target for maximum penetration.

I generally teach women to use their elbows in four different ways. The delivery is either upward, downward, forward or backward. In each delivery, the fist should be clenched loosely and tightened as the elbow nears its target. You should always focus through the target so that when you make contact, your elbow is moving at maximum speed. See Figures 7-41, 7-42 and 7-43.

Figure 7-41

Figure 7-42

Reach High
Use
Point of
Elbow

Figure 7-43

Pull Forward
Slam Head
Backward

Figure 7-44

Head Strike

The back of your head and upper portion of your forehead can be used to stun someone attacking you from behind or from directly in front respectively. Properly performing the neck stretching exercises can help you develop this technique. See Figure 7-44

Biting

I've been told that the human bite is tremendously powerful. Having seen circus performers dangled by their teeth and having been bitten a few times, I'm convinced.

Biting a man's fingers while they are clasped over your mouth or biting his neck while you are being bear-hugged from the front are easy for you to do, but are difficult for him to prevent and to endure. Biting a finger held over your mouth is not difficult, if you grab his hand

or arm and pull it down some. You may not have enough strength to pull his hand completely away from your mouth, but moving it just a little can enable you to bite a finger. See Figure 7-45.

Figure 7-45

While visiting St. Louis to present a general self-defense program for men and women, a participant showed me an article from a local paper which described how a woman bit off part of a rapist's tongue to put an end to his attack. It did.

I'm sure that somewhere down in the St. Louis area, a man may someday be overheard saying, "I thure did make a big mithake going afther her. She juth wathn't worth it." Every time I see a picture of Tweedy Bird, I think of St. Louis. See Figures 7-46 and 7-47.

Figure 7-46

Figure 7-47

G.S.T.P. Groin Strike

Although most of the techniques mentioned above can be directed toward the groin, this technique surpasses them all. Let's take a look at the acronym.

G - Grab the scrotum or the pouch of skin which holds the testicles and attempt to cup one or both of the testicles in your hand.

S - Squeeze the testicle in an attempt to crush or flatten it. If you have any doubt at all about your ability to do this, then let's put you through a convincing test. The cost will be the price of two Grade A large eggs and the time spent to hard boil them.

After peeling away the shell, place the eggs in a plastic bag which offers about as much protection as the thin skinned scrotum. OK - we're ready for the test. Hold the plastic bag in one hand and grab the simulated scrotum. Cup the testicle(s) and squeeze as hard as you can. Bingo. No more round shaped egg(s). No more testicle(s). The eggs are a mess and the rapist is hemorrhaging. You have completed the test and I have made my point.

T - Twist the "flattened" testicle. I threw this in because it is relatively easy to do, will help you grab hold of a testicle in case you have not, and it more than guarantees sufficient damage to your assailant.

P - Pull the mass in your hands (whatever is left) as hard as you can. Need I say more?

Note: A man's clothing will usually not protect him from this technique.

Also, if the rapist has overcome all of your defenses, then perhaps a little trickery is in store.

• If you are being forced to touch him, act as if you are going along with his wishes, and then do the G.S.T.P strike.

• If the scrotum cannot be grabbed, his penis can be targeted. One woman put it very simply, **"If you have control of it, he doesn't."**

Remember what the woman did in St. Louis when she bit the assailant's tongue.

Fake compliance, then attack.

Blocks

A situation may arise when an offensive technique is not an option. You may have to immediately use your arms for protection against an incoming fist or object. With that in mind, following are some blocks you can learn and develop.

Crossed Arm Block

If an assailant is swinging an object downward toward your head, this block can help protect you. Simply thrust both forearms toward the object with the palms facing away. One arm should be in front of the other, crisscrossing at about a forty degree angle. Clench the fists tightly and brace yourself against the blow.

Double Arm Block

Again, if an assailant is already swinging at you with his fist or object, and if stepping aside is not a possibility due to a lack of space or time, then this block may suffice. Place both arms in front of your face, parallel to each other. Allow enough space between to see your attacker. See Figure 7-48.

Figure 7-48

Full Body Block

This is an excellent technique to use when avoiding an incoming blow is difficult. The body and head are shifted away from the attack. The back hand is placed in front of the face with the open palm facing the attacker. The other arm is held closely against the side of the body with the hand positioned in a fist. If possible, the back leg should be bent and the front knee is lifted up to maximize full body protection. See Figure 7-49.

Figure 7-49

Incidentally, several offensive techniques can easily be delivered from this defensive position. You should be aware that blocks are most effective when immediately followed up with offensive techniques. When you practice blocking, you should always incorporate counterattack techniques. Always be thinking, "Block and counter, block and counter..."

Fakes/Set-ups

The situation might arise where an assailant needs to be tricked or baited before you counterattack. If you can get an opponent to commit to what he perceives is an attack or a retreat, chances are he will open himself up to a surprise attack.

For example, you could execute a back fist strike toward an assailant's face, not necessarily to hit him, but to simply draw his attention to your hand. Meanwhile, you are delivering a knee kick which he is totally unaware of.

Another example, is to act as if you are attempting to flee, stop suddenly, and deliver a technique toward your advancing assailant. Again, he will be preoccupied. If he has been concentrating on catching and grabbing you, he probably has not had much concern about being attacked himself. Sorry Charlie!

Combinations

Both traditional and contemporary martial arts training emphasize implementing hand and foot techniques in combinations to confuse, frustrate and overcome an opponent. I totally agree. You should continue defending until he stops his attack. Once his attack is stopped, get as far away from him as fast as you can. Nevertheless, remember that one technique may not necessarily stop him.

I suppose that is why I cringe every time someone says they carry their car keys in their closed fists for parking lot protection and will use them if necessary. They imply that the "ultimate" defense is already in hand. That clearly defines the phrase "wishful thinking." I always ask, "What would you do if the keys didn't stop him?"

Play it safe and if ever attacked, muster enough courage to bombard him with everything that you have. Combinations which you have repeatedly practiced can be performed without any hesitation. A series of techniques can be most difficult for an assailant to anticipate and block.

If you are soon perceived to be a kicking, biting, punching, jabbing, screaming and yelling "wild woman", then, you will not be seen as the easy prey he had envisioned.

PERSONAL TRAINING RECOMMENDATIONS

If you can set aside about three hours a week to practice the above mentioned stretches and techniques, you can develop enough flexibility and technical skills to keep yourself in a state of physical readiness.

Training with a friend usually works best. Following are some guidelines which will hopefully prove helpful.

Safety Precautions

1. Wear loose and comfortable clothing.

2. All stretching and self-defense techniques should be done in moderation.

3. Be sure to properly stretch and warm up the body before practicing techniques.

4. If working out with somebody, establish "no contact" rules.

5. Consult your doctor before beginning this or any kind of self-defense training.

Sample Workout

Stretching (5 minutes)

1. Perform the stretches which you have been introduced to.

2. Remember to start at the neck and work your way down.

3. All stretching should be done slowly.

4. Try to relax. Breathe slowly.

5. Never overextend.

6. Warm-up exercises such as running in place, sit-ups, jumping rope, etc. should be done at this point for approximately two minutes.

7. Be aware that **stretching after a workout** when the body is

warmed up **improves your flexibility.**

Blocks (2 minutes)

1. Perform 5-10 repetitions on each side.

- Full Body
- Crossed Arm
- Double Arm

2. Include sidestepping and head fades.

3. Concentrate more on the mechanics of the techniques than speed.

Hand Techniques (10 Minutes)

1. Unless striking a pad or bag, do not practice at full speed.

2. Concentrate on focusing your techniques at a specific target or area.

3. Remember to recover your fighting stance after completing each technique.

4. Within about 10 minutes, practice (10 repetitions on each side) as many of the following techniques you feel comfortable with.

- Back Fist
- Hammer Fist
- Y-Hand
- Palm Strike
- Finger/Thumb Gouge
- Elbow Strikes (vary which ones)

Kicking Techniques (10 minutes)

1. Practice the kicks slowly.

2. Do not overextend.

3. Concentrate on your focus.

4. Remember to recover to your original fighting stance.

5. Practice 10 repetitions of each kick or as many as possible within the time frame.

- Front Kick (Upward Thrust)
- Front Kick (Forward Thrust)
- Back Kick
- Side Kick
- Knee Strike (both upward and diagonal)

Combinations (10-15 minutes)

1. Give yourself plenty of room for these techniques.

2. Practice each combination you develop, slowly at first.

3. Visualize your attacker's presence.

4. Concentrate on proper technique.

Note: Give yourself a few minutes to gradually "cool down" as you complete the last few combinations. You have given yourself an aerobic, muscle toning workout and strengthened your self-defense skills simultaneously. Be fit and protected.

Time and money permitting, I do recommend that you explore some professional training at a reputable, affordable, well-organized and operated martial arts studio. Here are a few tips of what to look for:

1. Beware of programs which require you to sign an expensive multi-year or black belt contract. I recommend short commitments of one year or less. If the organization offers a significant discount for a longer commitment, it might prove to be worthwhile, but there is the possibility that you, or the school, might not be there very long.

2. Sports karate and kick boxing studios should be avoided if possible. I doubt that as a woman, your number one concern is to break bricks or have your nose broken in attempting to win a $15.00 trophy at a tournament. I believe that your interest lies in learning how to effectively protect yourself if a man is trying to abduct, rape or injure you. Stay focused on what you need most and find an organization that focuses on that need as well. Frankly, I have not found too many that do.

3. Don't make this decision in a hurry or when you are tired. This was a business tip which has been one of the best pieces of advice ever to come my way.

Chapter Eight - APPLIED LEARNING

In this chapter, some of the questions you were asked in chapter one (21-40) will be answered. Several tips on what to do in situations involving confined areas, parking lots and traveling will be offered. It is time to apply the principles and techniques discussed in earlier chapters. It is time to apply learning.

CONFINED AREA

21. You are alone in your home, motel, dormitory, etc., and you are suddenly confronted by an intruder whom you have never met. Surprised and frightened, a terrifying thought occurs to you. Let's assume that your intuition tells you that you are standing across the room from a rapist. There is no immediate means of escape. Without hesitation, he begins to lunge toward you. You have approximately one full second to respond. What would you do?

As mentioned earlier, I recommend that you do something drastic and surprising such as breaking a window, television screen or knocking over furniture. When you first pick up an object, it might be necessary to act as if you are going to throw it at him and then turn and break the window. Screaming and yelling is fine now that you have a chance of being heard. Broken glass or anything else within reach can be used as a weapon. Also, if he is still a few feet away, you can position yourself into the casual or fighting stance and prepare to kick at his knees.

Remember, if he is close, the elbows, knees, front kick (upward thrust) and some hand techniques can be used. Any object which can be used as a weapon should be picked up as well. You can call out a name. You can yell at him and tell him "Get out of here, get out! You are not going to get away with this!" Plan your escape and go for it.

22. Let's assume that you are in an identical predicament as mentioned above, except that the intruder is slowly walking toward you while trying to make some off-the-wall conversation. Again, you intuitively sense that the intruder has raping you on his mind. What would you do?

Do **not** take a chance. Follow the same steps mentioned above. You can limit your defense to a broken window and a few harsh words, a small price to pay for piece of mind.

23. You are alone in your home, motel, dormitory, etc., with a man who is an acquaintance. What began as a friendly and "normal" conversation, starts to change. To your surprise, your acquaintance is suddenly using sexually suggestive language. He is attempting to get close to you. Embarrassed and frightened, you begin to back away. What would you say to him?

I would be prepared to immediately follow the steps mentioned in question #1. However, if there is some room between you, and his advances are reserved and subtle, then he needs to hear a few words. Remember, your tone of voice, volume and delivery need to come across convincingly. Get loud and get crude. One suggestion is for you to say, "Listen, I don't know what you have on your mind, but this is not going to happen the way that you think." If you know the individual well, or have met friends or relatives of his, then I suggest you mention that "If this stops here, we'll forget it. If you continue, if you touch me, I'll tell your mother, the people at work, neighbors, etc. I'll tell everybody what you tried to do. This is not going to happen the way that you might think."

24. Concerning the above situation, what would you do if your verbal response failed to discourage his advances. Your "no" is not enough.

Follow the advise given to you in question #1. Make a strong effort to appear more angry then afraid. Anger suggests power whereas fear suggests vulnerability. Prepare to defend.

25. You are alone, lying on your back with a rapist sitting on top of you. Each of his hands is holding one of your's. His size and strength completely overpower you. It is abundantly clear to you that a disaster is only a few moments away. Feeling desperately helpless, you need to something. What would you do? Since 1988, I have been asking this question to women. Common answers include:

"I would take my knees and push him off me."

"I would tell him that I have AIDS."

"I would try to talk him out of it."

"I would throw up, wet my pants, or fake a seizure."

"I have no idea of what I would do."

"Nothing - I would be raped."

The problem with the above responses is that they are predictable and have probably been heard or seen by rapists before. If a man has you pinned to the ground and he has superior strength, leverage, and fighting ability, what can you do? For all practical purposes, nothing. There really isn't anything that you can do at that point. But on the flip side, let me ask you another question. What can he do? Nothing. Both of his hands are holding your hands. In order for him to disrobe, fondle or abuse you, he has to let go of one of your hands. Even if he has a knife to your throat or a gun to your head, usually these weapons are used to simply set the stage and terrorize you into compliance. Typically, the weapon will be placed aside while the rape continues. The point is that he will in some way have to temporarily free up your hands. Even if he is trying to tie your hands, a moment might arise where you have a chance to do something. Incidentally, do anything that you can to avoid being bound. If need be, revert to some tricks. Let him know that you can do more for him untied, etc.

Essentially, what you have to do is wait for the right opportunity. It will present itself. He will be vulnerable at one time or another. Unfortunately and understandably, I think what often happens with women who are in this predicament, is that they tend to lose control psychologically and emotionally. In their mind they think, "I've got to get out of here. No, this can't happen. Somebody help me. I've got to do something . . . " etc. A panic condition can take over and we know what happens then. The crux of the matter is that you cannot do anything. Force yourself (as difficult as it might be) to wait for an opportunity. Then, quickly exploit his vulnerabilities.

The time to strike is when an opportunity presents itself.

- Martial Arts Motto

When the opportunity is there, you have to maximize the results of everything that you do. The techniques to the throat, the G.S.T.P. groin strike, elbow strikes, biting, eye strikes, etc. must be used with every bit of energy that you can muster. It is the decisive moment. Seize it!

26. You have opened a door in your home, motel, dormitory, etc. and as you begin to enter, someone grabs you from behind and is attempting to push you inside. He is holding you with one hand and covering your mouth with the other. He orders you to go inside. Would you cooperate? If not, what would you do?

A simple rule of thumb is that you never go to a designated area which an assailant is directing you to. Rapists fear audiences and there is a definite reason he wants you to himself. If someone has his hand over your mouth, the first thing that you need to do is to grab his arm. With one or both of your arms, quickly pull his arm downward. Even if you can only pull his arm down one-half of an inch, that will suffice. As you are pulling on his arm to lower his hand, simultaneously attempt to bite one or more of his fingers. He will probably assume that you are trying to scream, and will probably not be expecting the bite. Also, if need be, fall to the ground. Do anything to slow the process. Many self-defense techniques which you have been introduced to will work in this situation.

27. You are alone and in bed sleeping. Breaking glass, a door being pushed in, a door lock being jimmied, etc., alerts you to the fact that someone is

trying to enter your dwelling. What would you do?

If you have a gun, get it and be prepared to use it. If there is a door separating you and the area where you heard the noise, shut it and lock it. If you live in an apartment or house which has neighbors close by, break a window and scream. Pick up the phone and call 911. Tell them that someone is in your house. Position yourself so that as he comes through the door, you have all the advantages including the element of surprise. If there is another way to exit away from the sound, try that.

The important point for you to remember is that you must do something. Don't stand there hoping that it will all go away. Call a man's name as if waking somebody up. If you are alone with one or more children, your first concern should be to protect them as well as yourself. Quickly grab the gun and perform what police departments call "clearing an area." Walk with the gun facing toward the floor or the ceiling and begin to check the house out as you approach your children's room. Loudly wake them up and tell them to run toward your bedroom. Hopefully, you can hoard your children behind you in the bedroom before facing the intruder. Shut the bedroom door, order your children to lay down on the floor, and prepare to shoot the intruder should he burst into the room. Do not leave the room until the police arrive.

Make an effort to ensure that the police officers responding to your call know that you are in the bedroom. Open the window or break it to attract their attention. Leaving the bedroom may give the intruder an opportunity to grab you and either silence you or use you as a hostage. Besides, the police officers will most likely be "clearing" the house themselves. Stay in your refuge.

Incidentally, the clearing technique can be used if you think you may have heard something, but are not sure. You might not feel comfortable calling the police every time you hear a noise, but turning on a few lights and clearing the area with your gun may give you a piece of mind. This situation is one reason why I endorse alarm systems.

One other situation could arise whereby someone is ringing your doorbell or knocking on the door. If it is late in the evening or early in the morning, be especially careful and suspect. If your porch light is not on, then turn it on. Having your gun in hand is a good idea. If you can see the individual through a peep hole or window, take note of his description. Do not answer the door. If he continues to knock, immediately call the police or a neighbor. A few words such as, "Dave, can you get it?" or "Gary, there's someone at the front door." may deter your un-wanted guest. You may want to say, "Go ahead, keep knocking. The police are on the way." Loudly tell the man that you have called the police and take refuge in the corner of a room with a telephone nearby. If you have a panic button on an alarm system, and sense that this guy is not going to go away, use it.

You should also be aware, particularly in condominiums and apartments that a soft, quiet knock may suggest the pres-ence of someone who is trying to gain entry without attracting the attention of others. Some-one knocking at your door may also be a way of distracting you while someone else enters an-other part of the house. Listen for other noises and position yourself away from in front of the door. If the person at your door hears your voice directly behind the door, he knows that if he can burst through the door, then you are within grabbing distance. He knows that you will not have ample time to react. He hopes that you are not armed and trusting the strength of the door to protect you. Keep him guessing and distance your-self. Position yourself where you can monitor both the door and other parts of the home. If pos-sible, stay on the phone with the police. If your phone is out of or-der, and someone is knocking on your front door, be even more careful and prepared.

28. Gang rape in which a victim is abused by several assailants, is often perceived by women as the most horrifying and traumatic experience imaginable. Women have de-scribed it as the ultimate nightmare. If you were in a con-fined area with several men and sensed that the chances of be-ing gang raped were increasing, what would you do to calm the tide? If the men started fondling and forcing themselves upon you, what would you do?

Unfortunately, gang rape is not only a horrifying experience, but it is also the most difficult to defend against. You should al-ways avoid situations where you are the only woman with a group of men (acquaintances or strangers). Especially avoid those who are becoming more vulgar, aggressive and jokingly sexual. The best advice that I can offer you is to nip it in the bud. When you detect danger signs of things getting out of control, make your move early to dispel any hopes and aspira-tions. If you are consuming anything which can affect your awareness and coherence, be aware that you will be viewed as easier prey. For all practical pur-poses, you will be. Drugs and/or alcohol can raise some serious concerns in the realm of con-sent. Linda Fairstein, a Manhattan district attorney in charge of the sex-crimes unit was quoted in Time magazine as saying "The defense will say she gave consent and just doesn't remember." (Time Aug. 23, 1987). The rape will just become part of the ol' party. You won't have enough control of yourself or them to do anything about it. Later it will be the word of many against your word, which at the time of the attack, was somewhat slurred.

Remember, the distraction techniques such as breaking a window or anything else for that matter. Making the room look like a war zone can cause some gang members to question how far they want to pursue the idea of raping you. If you can make the situation look ugly, the "gang-banging" will not have the same appeal. Hopefully, it will appear more criminal.

Look for people in the room who appear to be stable. Inform them you are not willing, nor oblivious to what is about to happen. Let it be known that everything and everyone will be remembered and that it will become public record at any cost. Should one or more of the men begin to physically assault you, then do what I have always been taught. Make an example of the first person who touches you. Put all your effort into hurting him as quickly and severely as you can. Gouging eyes, biting and groin grabs can be convincing. As a young boy, I remember someone pointing out an older kid from the neighborhood with the comment that "he was nothing to mess with." I wasn't particularly impressed with the teenager's size or demeanor and was curious why he merited such neighborhood re-

spect. Later I was informed that the teenager, when attacked by several youths his age, clamped his teeth on the cheek of the first youth who attempted to hurt him. Like a pitbull, he refused to loosen his grip. His convincing commitment to prevail and the screaming youth's bleeding cheek apparently changed some minds and intentions.

You have to inflict pain and do some damage. You have to convince the men beyond any doubt, that the party will not go on as planned. The party is over.

PARKING LOTS

29. What do you typically do to safeguard against abduction or rape when exiting a building or your home and approaching your vehicle?

Parking lot routines have already been discussed. Allow me to modify some of these steps and include some of my own.

A. I think it is a good idea to have your car key ready but not visible. If a rapist spots you in a large mall for example, he will want to verify whether you are by yourself. Unless he saw you pull up in your car, he couldn't necessarily determine that. After all, someone you were with could be shopping elsewhere with plans of rendezvousing shortly. How would he know for sure?

He will know you are by your-self the moment you take your car keys out.

The problem is that most women take their car keys out before they leave a building. All I'm saying is that it is perfectly fine to have your car keys easily accessible, just don't broadcast that to the whole world. Placing a plastic identifying cover over the handle portion of the car key will make feeling for the key in a pocket a breeze. Such devices are available at most hardware stores.

B. As you are leaving the building, take just a moment to look over your shoulder and see if anybody is directly behind you or standing a short distance away watching you. If some guy is there and you are not comfortable having him follow you toward your car, stop and let him pass by. Waiting ten seconds to exit a store or building will not ruin your day. This gives you an opportunity to check him out. If it is a false alarm, oh well, ten seconds lost. If possible, exit the building with others or look for people (preferably men and women) entering their vehicles as well.

C. As you walk toward your car, hold your purse close to you. Walk down the center of an aisle whenever possible. Glance around as you walk and use your senses to check out the area. It doesn't hurt to glance

under your vehicle as you ap-proach it. Remember, an individual may not be positioned right there near your car. See Figure 8-1.

Figure 8-1

He may time his attack so that when you near your destination, so does he. Some people rec-ommend that you walk confidently. I recommend that you simply give the impression that you are totally aware of your surroundings. If a car pulls up close to you, be sure to im-mediately look toward the car to see if anyone is exiting. Glance around and see if anyone is suddenly approaching you and the car. See Figure 8-2.

Figure 8-2

Keep in mind an accomplice might be in the area to simply grab and shove you in the car so that all the driver has to do is press down on the accelerator. If the car slows up next to you, either move a few steps back or a few steps forward, so that anyone jumping out of the car cannot simply grab you on the spot. This is especially important if a van or a car with more than one occupant is approaching.

There is nothing wrong with you stopping and looking over your shoulder as you approach your vehicle. It is not a bad idea, particularly if you sense that something is amiss, to stop at the car next to yours, get your car key out and to scout out the area. The assailant, if he did attack you at that point, would not necessarily know that this is not your car. If his plans were to abduct you in your own vehicle (usually the case), then he is in for a surprise.

Periodically pausing and looking behind yourself in a parking lot protects you and "wastes" only a few seconds at best.

KEEP HIM GUESSING!!!

D. As you reach your vehicle, practice what I call my last minute observation technique. Take just a moment before opening your trunk or car door to look over your left and right shoulder. From the research that I have done, if someone is going to come out of nowhere, this is when you will probably see him. See Figure 8-3.

Figure 8-3

E. If you are forced to put personal belongings in the car such as shopping bags, brief case, purse, etc., then pause periodically to see if someone is approaching while you are apparently preoccupied.

F. Prior to entering your vehicle, lock your doors with your power door lock button if you have one or lock the driver's side door. This way, all doors are locked once you shut the door behind you.

G. If your vehicle will not start (God forbid), wait until you see enough people that you are comfortable with before leaving the car. If someone is at the window insisting that you open the door and your unwillingness to do so isn't working, lay on the horn and turn the lights off and on until he gets the message.

Ask for help back in the building, but not from some kind-looking man who just happens to appear out in the parking lot. The sudden mechanical failure of your car may be the result of tampering. A Johnnie-on-the-spot mechanic may be a setup.

30. As you are opening the door of your vehicle, you notice that someone is lunging at you. The assailant is approximately six to eight feet away, at the back of your vehicle. Incidentally this is most advantageous for the assailant. He knows you probably won't see him until the last moment. He knows you cannot run toward the front of your vehicle since your opened car door is in the way. He knows that you will probably try to enter and lock your vehicle before he gets to you. You have less than one second in which to attempt some kind of defense. What would it be?

Well, you have more time to think about this than my sister had. I have listened and read what others have recommended at this point. As mentioned before, everyone seems to favor using the keys as a weapon. Most martial artists will recommend some particular fighting technique. Not me. I'll tell you what you ought to do.

Get away from that car door immediately. If you have to throw groceries at the assailant, slam the door or stumble backward, so be it. Get away from that door! If he is only a few feet away, I highly doubt that you will be able to enter and lock your vehicle before he intervenes. Just remember that if you decide to do anything else, it better work. If it doesn't, he has you exactly where he wants you to be.

Once you step away from the door, be prepared to **do something worthwhile with those keys, get rid of them**. Throw them under the car next to you or across the parking lot. Once you have discarded the keys, you have limited the options available to him. At least, he cannot simply push you in the car, and with your keys, drive away with his victim. He must either attempt to rape you right there next to your car in the middle of the parking lot (which he probably will not do), or he must attempt to drag you toward your car only to find out that the car door is locked. His only other option is to then drag you back to his vehicle. His attack will not be going as he had planned.

Remember too, once you have stepped back and thrown the keys, you still have distanced yourself enough to use some self-defense techniques presented earlier. If you are a believer in mace, pepper spray or CS tear gas canisters, you have enough time to prepare to spray.

Parking garages are particularly dangerous. They are usually poorly lit, often unattended, seldom monitored and have virtually unlimited places for assailants to hide. My advice for you is to never walk toward your car without having a trusted acquaintance with you. Don't do it. Ask a security guard to accompany you or wait for others to enter the area.

Moreover, if you habitually leave work with other employees and park in elevated or underground garages, agree to meet at the exit before leaving the premises. If your friend doesn't show up by the designated time, simply go for help or drive back to see if there is a problem.

31. About the above situation, how would you respond if the assailant were simply walking toward you and attempting to make conversation?

Listen dear reader, he might be a loving father of six children, grandfather of two, a church officer and his neighborhood's favorite citizen. Perhaps he is genuinely interested in helping you lift something into your back seat or finding out where a particular street is. Of course, he could be a Ted Bundy type with evil intentions and a personality and appearance which could fool the world. The problem is that given a few seconds, you need the diagnostic skills of a clinical psychologist and the luck of an experienced poker player to decide whether the situation is "safe."

You can't take a chance on being wrong. Back away from the door anyway. Since the individual is walking, and not lunging at you, there is enough time to tactfully and casually step back a step or two. Incidentally, once this guy (assuming he is a dirtbag) sees you step away, he will probably sense that he has been "spotted." At that point, his street smarts usually come into play in that he will attempt to make conversation to get near you. Be careful. In essence, what you are doing by stepping back and defining "your space" is silently communicating to him that "Hey, I don't have a problem talking to you, but if you are who you say you are, talk to me from there." If he is the nice guy, so what? He will get over it.

You simply cannot take a chance. Some people might label this technique as a little overboard or paranoid. Given the high crime rate in our country, particularly with the alarming number of car jackings, I consider it prudent and sensible. I would rather have you safe than to have you sorry.

If the individual continues to advance toward you, after you have backed up and communicated your preference toward long distance communication, beware. When I intentionally distance myself from a threatening individual, I watch for him to cross that imaginary line in coming toward me. The demilitarized zone has been violated. It most likely suggests time for evasive action. Think about the systematic self-defense system in this situation. You have discerned that the man could be dangerous. Backing away from your car door as you lock and close it will perhaps distract him. His continued advance helps your discernment. The keys are discarded (distraction). Scream or call somebody's name to attract others(distraction). Run if possible (depart). If you can't run, stand your ground. Position yourself in a fighting stance and prepare to defend. Then you depart.

32. As you are entering your vehicle in a crowded parking lot, a man suddenly enters the passenger side door, grabs you and orders you to back the car up and drive in a certain direction. He places a weapon against your side with a stern warning that any resistance will be dealt with immediately. He expects you to cooperate. Would you? If not, what would you do? This is a tough one isn't it?

I recommend that you stay with our little rules. Do not allow anyone to take you from point A to point B. True, if you do not do what he says, there is a question of what he will do at point A. On the other hand, there is the same question of what he will do to you later (at point B) if you obey his commands. In my mind, both pose some serious

concerns but what he will do at point B seems to pose the biggest concern. Unless he is completely deranged, he recognizes some restrictions on what he can do in a crowded parking lot. What he will do to you once he has you away from others with no apparent limiting restrictions is another story. Too many women abducted are never seen again. Too many women who oblige are no longer alive to tell you about it. If he is carrying the AIDS virus, he is killing you anyway isn't he? He is less prepared to kill you now than he will be later.

I recommend that you call his hand to see his cards. Careful not to hit anybody, back the car up into a car behind you. Ram the car into a barrier or light pole. Lay on the horn. Turn the car off, pull the keys out and throw them in the back seat or quickly open the door and get rid of the keys. Now you have forced him to go to a plan B which is something he might not have anticipated. Guess who is probably panicking now? I do not think he will rape, shoot or knife you in a crowded parking after the car has been seemingly immobilized.

Win, lose or draw, at least you have changed the rules and have given yourself a chance. It should be mentioned that due to the circumstances, you might be forced to temporarily fake compliance and immobilize the car at another time, such as when you spot a police car or see several people in an area.

33. You are carrying a purse and a shopping bag and as you approach your vehicle, a van pulls up next to you. A man quickly exits and is reaching toward you in what is an apparent abduction attempt. What would you do?

Throw the bags at him. A natural reaction is for him to block or attempt to catch them. This buys you valuable time. Distance yourself and run if possible or prepare to defend.

TRAVELING

34. While walking, jogging or bicycling, someone grabs you in a bear-hug from behind and is attempting to drag you behind some bushes or into a vehicle which suddenly pulls up.

You need to do something to prevent the abduction and probable rape. What would you do?

I came up with a technique in 1986, which I later used in a combination for a martial arts test in 1988. I can tell you from personal experience that the technique works. I wish my sister had known this technique when she was grabbed. Usually when I speak to an audience at a company, school or church, I ask for a volunteer to accompany me. I assure the participant that no harm will come their way, and inform them of what I will (in slow--motion) do to them.

I have them face the audience. I come up from behind and grab the person in a bearhug. I let the audience know that this is exactly how my sister was attacked. As I am standing there holding onto the participant, I ask her to lift up the lower parts of her arms. Although her upper arms (from the elbow upward) are held tightly, she can still move the lower arms.

After I have proved that some movement of the arms is still possible, I ask the woman to slowly cross one foot over the other. As she places the one foot over the other, I stop and ask the audience what she has done by taking the step. I have heard people respond by guessing that she had regained her balance or thrown him off balance.

I start over and have the woman go through the steps again. The question is again asked and participants usually have this "I don't know - tell me" look on their faces. So I do. I let them know that when a woman crosses one leg over the other, she opens the attacker's groin.

She would never think of hitting him there because her own body is in the way. I always make it a habit of reminding the audience that I repeated the movement twice in slow-motion and no one, absolutely no one, detected what was being accomplished by the movement. If they didn't know what was going on, I do not think a rapist would either. I further instruct that once the step is taken, a woman needs to lift up her arm (which has been previously shown) as much as possible, and begin to thrust her hand back toward the man's groin area. The audience is instructed to tighten the hand into a clenched fist as it nears the target. Ouch! Audiences just love this technique. Next, I instruct the participant to tilt her head forward and touch her chin on her chest and then immediately thrust the head backward into the man's facial area. Ouch! Participants are instructed to perform both techniques one right after the other.

It would be most difficult for an attacker to anticipate both techniques, must less to block them. Double ouch!! The techniques should be continued until the assailant lets go.

35. As you are entering a motel lobby, you are reminded of the predicament awaiting you. You are traveling alone and will be locking yourself into a room in a few minutes. Unfortunately, every time this happens, there is usually some anxiety involved. You are never quite sure whether someone is lurking behind the shower curtain or under the bed. You are either locking an unwelcome visitor out or locking one in with you. What could you do to alleviate these anxious moments?

A couple of things come to mind. First, you should try to check in at the front desk when a crowd is not present. Ask for an inner room where there is no door facing the outside of the motel. Sometimes with busy motels and hotels this is impossible. If the desk clerk hands you your room key and states the room number loud enough for the entire room full of people to hear, quietly ask for another room and ask him to be a little more discreet. You could ask the front desk to have a member of the staff accompany you to your room. The larger and more expensive hotel chains might be equipped with enough staff to help you in this matter.

Another suggestion is for you to ask the attendant at the front desk to do you a special and important favor. Inform him that you are going directly to your room and will be calling him back in less than five minutes. Further inform him that if the call is not made, that you would appreciate him sending someone to your room. At least this way, when you go up to your room and lock the door behind you, you can check out the room with a little more peace of mind. If it is your misfortune to have someone hiding in the room, you have the systematic defense system you can use, and, unbeknown to him, you have someone coming up to your room if that phone call is not made.

Also, if someone is following you in a motel hallway, stop between rooms and allow the individual to pass. Standing near the door of your room is not a good idea. Remember, individuals can time their approach toward you so that they arrive just in time to execute their plan.

Have you ever noticed in some hotels that the bellboy will set your suitcases down and then check out the bathroom? Let me ask a question. Is he routinely checking for soap in the shower or is he performing a mini-security check which management knows is not a bad idea?

36. You are alone and waiting for an elevator to stop at your floor. A man walks up behind you. The elevator door opens and the man politely motions for you to enter before him. No one else is in the area. You are uncomfortable with his suggestion, but since you are not any more at ease in a vacant hallway, you decide to enter the elevator. Where would you stand in relation to where he positions himself?

I believe that most women are not really too comfortable riding elevators by themselves or with a stranger. Most people are unusually quiet and tense when forced to travel with others in such a confined area. Everyone's "space" is violated. The entertainment industry has often depicted victims trapped in an elevator, fleeing from somebody in one, or desperately waiting for a door to open.

Concerning the above question, I recommend that you enter the elevator only if you feel more "safe" in it then waiting in the hallway for it to come back. But if you do enter the elevator, I recommend that you stand near the control buttons and turn so that the man, wherever he stands, can be seen out of the corner of your eye. See Figure 8-4.

Figure 8-4

As always, be prepared to implement any or all techniques via the systematic self-defense system. One advantage that you do have in such a confined area is that most elevators have an arm rest or guard rail on each wall. If you did have to execute a kick for example, you can brace yourself on the arm rest or guard rail and deliver a powerful and well balanced technique. See Figure 8-5.

Figure 8-5

The elevator buttons and phone can help you as well. I contacted the Detroit Elevator Company which has been repairing elevators for over 78 years. I asked them about stop and emergency buttons on both old and new elevators. According to that company, the older elevators have stop buttons which if depressed, will immediately stop the elevator. Unfortunately, most of the older models (25 or more years old) do not activate any type of alarm when this occurs. Some do not have emergency buttons and the phones may not have automatic dialers. Stuck between floors in one of these could create a problem.

A hand-held sounding device could prove helpful in a confined area. Keep in mind however, that you do have your voice and as any elevator repairman will tell you, sounds are easily heard between floors on an elevator. I went to a department store and had my wife remain next to the elevator while I rode it two floors down. Risking embarrassment, I talked and yelled all the way. She could hear me just fine. You can always scream and yell. Modern elevators, particularly those satisfying city codes, have some type of emergency sounding device (bell or siren) which is activated when either the emergency or stop buttons are pressed. Even if there is a power failure, these systems have a backup power pack for the sounding devices. Emergency phones usually have automatic dialers which means that if attacked, you only need to somehow pick up the phone and to call for help. No dialing is necessary.

If someone is forcing you to accompany him to a particular floor such as a top floor or basement, then you know as we have discussed earlier that he is trying to isolate you. You cannot let that happen. Play by your rules, not his. Do anything in your power to stop the elevator, defend and distract.

37. While driving alone at night on an expressway, your car suddenly stalls. You are forced to make an emergency stop. What would you do to safeguard against any danger and to also summon assistance?

First, your car doors should already be locked. Immediately turn on your emergency flashers. If you have a mobile phone, call the police and report your approximate location and ask for assistance. After you have called the police, call for automotive service. Remember later to use your mobile phone to confirm whether the police car or tow truck behind you is legitimate.

If a police car pulls up behind you, look for the following:

• Police cars will generally shine an additional spot light on your car or will have their flashers on.

Chapter Eight - APPLIED LEARNING

- The officer should be in full dress uniform.

If a tow truck pulls up behind you, perform the following checklist:

- The towing vehicle should have its flashers on.

- Ask for identification.

- Exit your vehicle only when you are completely comfortable in doing so.

If a car pulls up behind you and a man approaches you to offer assistance, make sure your doors are locked (they should always be), and do not roll down the window. Inform him that your husband is on his way back, help is on the way, etc. If the man is sensitive to your security needs and is willing to work on the engine without having you open the car door or window, well maybe. But under no circumstances do you unlock that door or roll down that window.

If the man does start to pound on the driver's side window or attempt to break it, immediately move over to the other side of the seat and prepare to exit. You should be aware that a car window can be shattered quite easily. A man can place a small steel dowel shaped object between his fingers and by simply slapping your window, shatter it and grab you or your purse.

Sound the horn and flash the lights. If you have a car alarm with a panic button, press it. If not, turn on the alarm system so that if a door is opened, the siren will be activated. If you have a cellular phone, hopefully you have already called for help. At any rate, inform the attacker that police have been called. Car phones and car alarms are extremely valuable items to have when it comes to rape prevention. Find a way to afford them. Squeeze personal safety into your budget.

Above and beyond any self-defense techniques, look for an object which can be used as a weapon. This will be discussed further in the next chapter which examines personal protection devices.

38. You are driving down a highway with a median dividing two lanes on each side. You are maintaining an average speed of approximately 45 miles per hour in the outside lane. You have noticed that a car has been following you closely. It pulls up alongside. The two male occupants are taunting you and motioning for you to pull over. What would you do?

You can ignore them and hope that their taunting will diminish or cease. I know that if you are a woman who has been driving for some time, you have probably already experienced something like this. Sometimes the situation is less extreme. A car will simply pull up next to you and hold the same speed so that the occupant(s) can stare at you. You should be aware however that this situation can be more dangerous than it appears. Perhaps the occupant(s) are testing you and waiting for an opportune time to run you off the road.

If you sense that the situation is getting out of hand, you should find a way to maneuver your car into the inside lane. You may have to change your speed to do this. Do not slow up too much in order to do this however. Trying to pull you over in the inside lane is probably not as appealing as running you off into a ditch, curb, etc. If an opportunity arises where you can suddenly turn off from either lane onto another street, do so, but make sure that the street does not further isolate you from other traffic or pedestrians. Flashing your lights or putting on your emergency lights can help draw attention to your plight. Also, the car phone can be most intimidating and useful at this time. If possible, write down the license plate number. If the car is trying to force you off the road, then hold the steering tightly and accelerate. Your front fender will strike their vehicle and will most likely continue forward. Keep the accelerator floored and move over into the inside lane. Do not allow them to box you in again.

39. You are driving home and notice that someone might be following you. Since you have a few more miles before reaching your destination, you decide to verify whether your suspicion is correct. What would you do?

I recommend that you think of your immediate safety first. Everything else is secondary. I know others recommend you should not drive directly to your place of residence since this may be what he is trying to verify. But I have to tell you that if someone wants to find out where you live, that is not a difficult thing to do. For all practical purposes, you might as well assume that if there is someone out there wanting to know where you rest your head, it is really a no-brainer to determine that. In some states, Secretary of State offices release information to interested persons who submit a license plate number. If they have your plate number, it is only a matter of time before they have your address. Someone can also follow you a short distance one day, wait for you the next, follow a little further as days go by, until your residence is discovered. It might take some time, but it can be done. None of us live in a shell so don't worry about something which you just cannot have absolute control over. Just make sure that you are always on guard and prepared.

Since your personal safety for the moment is of primary concern, drive home if that is where immediate help is available. Pull up in the driveway and sound your horn, flash your lights, activate your car alarm, etc. However, if you see people out in front of a house, apartment, business, etc., then it might be a good idea to find immediate help there. Rapists do not like audiences. Try to get a description of the car, license number or occupant(s). Use your car phone and make sure that he can see you calling. Do not allow him an opportunity to pull you over even if he has bumped into the back of your car. You can report the minor collision to the police later and explain why you did not want to stop. **Do not leave your vehicle.**

Since we're on the topic of police, you need to be aware of something. Impersonating a police officer is not that difficult to do. While attending a class for reserve police officers, I was told by a guest speaker from a local police department that an individual was arrested in a neighboring community. Police officers confiscated a wig, police uniform, badge, identification, nylon stocking, drugging paraphernalia, weapons and other related items. Although the uniform was makeshift, the police officer was impressed how authentic everything appeared. I wonder how many women he fooled?

Consequently, if you are ever pulled over by a car with the little flashing light, remember a few things:

• Police officers usually try to pull vehicles over in lighted areas for obvious reasons. If this is not happening when it easily could be, then just be aware of the fact that something could be amiss.

• Portable red or blue flashing lights can be purchased without difficulty.

• Masquerading is not difficult (above example). Police and security guard uniforms can be bought or made with a little ingenuity.

• If a police officer pulls you over and asks for identification and you sense that something is wrong and out of place, then act on that intuition. Open your window enough to slide your license and registration through. If asked to exit the vehicle, ask the officer if that is absolutely necessary since you are not comfortable in doing so. If he insists, ask him if he wouldn't mind calling for a backup vehicle. Listen, I am not suggesting that anyone break the law here, I am just trying to protect women in what can often be a potentially dangerous situation. Any professional and legitimate police officer will understand your concerns and will do what he can to limit your fears. Again, if you have a car phone, call 911 and see if a patrol car has been dispatched to your location. Another option is to volunteer to follow him to a police station.

40. Unfortunately, when traveling on expressways after dark, you sometimes need to use a restroom. Since the women's rooms in rest stop areas are usually a lonely place at night, and since gas station restrooms are generally located around the side of a building, what precautionary steps can you take to safeguard yourself?

If possible, avoid using rest stops. If you must, use rest stop facilities where families are present, or where there are several men who do not appear to be together. If you pull up to a rest stop and notice a family parked near you, and the area is deserted, it would not hurt to ask them (if they will be there for a few moments) to make sure you return shortly. Most people would understand such a request.

In gas stations, when you ask to use the restroom and are given a key, inform the attendant in a tactful manner, "Ah, I'll be back in a few minutes. If not, I'm in trouble." Say whatever you feel comfortable saying, but let him or her know in one way or another, that you are not camping out in there and plan to return in a short time. I truly believe that most people are good and decent individuals. Most people are willing to help, if you ask them. Unfortunately, assuming that people will spontaneously look out for you is probably expecting too much.

This chapter offers a collection of personal protection ideas, recommendations, devices and a collection of stories to supplement and strengthen your rape prevention system. I decided to include information on how to avoid and overcome sexual harassment. This problem is a form of rape by itself and often leads to sexual abuse. Also, since children are often the targets of rape and some form of sexual assault, I thought that some readers would appreciate a few tips for tots.

TIPS FOR TOTS

My heart goes out to every mother and father whose child has disappeared due to apparent abduction. Potato chip bags, milk cartons, flyers in the mail, newspaper articles, television programs and radio news remind us daily to keep a closer eye on our children. Recently, Michigan has been bombarded with heartbreaking news concerning the disappearance, rape and murder of several children, teenagers and women. When I stop at the street corner nearest to my mother's house, I am approximately 200 yards away from the home where a girl was abducted in May 1993 from a slumber party and found battered to death two months later. A home video segment was shown on local news programs and a flyer was distributed to businesses all over neighboring cities.

That little girl was stolen away, raped and murdered. Her parents spent two agonizing months waiting for the phone to ring and praying with others for the safe return of their daughter. Eventually the phone did ring, but the message broke their hearts.

A 40 minute drive from my home will place me in the general area where Leslie Williams kidnaped, raped and murdered several young women. Reportedly, before the attacks, Williams had been recently released from prison after serving only a small part of his sentence. I'll give you two seconds to guess why he was incarcerated. Bzzz. Time's up. He was convicted of rape. A few weeks after Williams was arrested and brought to trial, I was interviewed by Bill Proctor, a local television reporter for WXYT - Channel 7 News. The television station had contacted me to see if I would be willing to give some personal protection tips for women and children. Fortunately, I was allowed to mention the idea of breaking windows in confined areas and throwing keys in parking lots. I wish I could have spoken for thirty minutes. One comment which was not aired involved William's early release due to good behavior. Good behavior? Wait a minute! I think I view things differently than parole boards. I understand that some individuals can turn their life around and after psychological counseling,

Chapter Nine - TIPS AND TALES

treatment and a true repentance (my criteria) - be ready to go back out in society. The problem is - how can you be sure? Frankly, I am sick and tired of reading about repeated sexual offenders serving ridiculously short sentences; then, being set free only to commit the same atrocities. Remember the statistics in chapter four? His good behavior freed him. Good behavior??? How else did they expect him to act? There were no women or children in that prison.

The point is this. Our children are not as protected as they should be nor have they been properly trained to protect themselves. There are more like Leslie Williams out there. Deanna Seiffert was abducted in her teddy bear night gown while spending the night at a slumber party. It can happen anytime and anywhere. Listen to me - learn from the animal world. Their young seldom leave their sight until they can adequately protect themselves. When it comes to protecting your children, that is my position exactly. I don't care what your day's agenda is, their protection is pre-eminent. When I talk to parents during rape-prevention seminars, I always remind them that "things are not what they used to be." As a child, I was gone for hours. Sexual crimes were not as prevalent and I was taught at home and in school how to avoid being a victim of crime in general. The crux of the matter is that our society today is much more violent and sexual crimes have increased significantly. To compound the problem, parents and schools are teaching what I was taught in the mid-fifties when it comes to avoiding abduction and rape.

Don't you think criminals, rapists in particular, are more creative and crafty now then thirty years ago? You bet your life they are. Telling children not to talk to strangers or take a piece of candy from a man in a car worked well for another generation. You need to read an article in the April 1992 edition of Redbook magazine entitled "How I Seduce a Child" - a Convicted Molester's Warning." Ross M. Nelson, currently serving a 20-year sentence in a Texas prison states that "For more than 40 years, I was a loving friend to hundreds of little boys. I took them fishing, helped them with homework, and listened to their problems. Their parents never suspected I was also having sex with them." The article details how he systematically and methodically lured his victims and sexually abused them for as long as he saw fit. Recently "Prime Time", a weekly television program, graphically illustrated how easily a child, even if forewarned of "strangers", can be deceived and led away in public areas. A man with the cooperation of each child's parents, acted as if he was looking for his lost puppy. He, along with a dog leash and a photograph of the missing puppy, would approach each child, or group of children, and ask if they had seen "Spot." He would then ask if each child would help him find the dog. Within moments, after short circuiting the children's defenses, he would have them following him away from others calling out for the dog.

Make certain that your children do not have a preconceived notion that "strangers" are strictly evil looking, monstrous, scary and threatening individuals. A "stranger" should be described as anyone you do not know, who is attempting to get you to go away from others or from where you have been told to stay.

Incest is another enormous problem in this country. I suspect that no one really knows how extensive this problem really is. Since the sexual attacks are perpetrated by "family" members, children should be taught early on that no one, Mommy, Daddy, brother, sister, etc. is allowed to touch private parts. The children must be taught that saying "NO" to anyone, running, screaming, "telling on others" are all unconditionally acceptable. Share this information with your children.

SAFETY ZONES

Your child is safe when you are there or if they are in an area which is not open to the public. Most parents of small

children tell them "Now Nicole, Johnny, etc., you know the rules. You cannot go out in the street. You can play in front, but you cannot go past the Hendrickson's house or the Milton's." Sometimes mom or dad is there, and sometimes not. Parents often assume that neighbors will somehow be watching.

Let me ask you a question. Do you think the parent(s) of a small child would allow it to play in a well-defined area one mile from home? They would not. Why? Most parents think that the area in front of their house is some kind of safety zone. They hope that someone will be around if the child needs protection. What if the phone rings and mother goes to answer it? What if the neighbor leaves his front porch to refill his iced tea glass?. What if Johnny or Nicole is there alone and a car with Ricky the Rapist in it suddenly turns the corner? What difference does it make if your child is there or one mile away? In Ricky's mind, there is no difference. Explain this to your children; they are trusting you to define "safe" for them.

SYSTEMATIC SELF-DEFENSE SYSTEM

It is common knowledge that children with early academic training seem to excel better than others. Moreover, most world class athletes started in their profession at a young age.

We are all aware how important it is to get an early start in life. Young minds are powerful, so in conjunction with everything else, teach them how to protect their body. Teach them the following tips concerning the five D's.

Discern

• A vehicle slowing up nearby or a stranger approaching on foot should be simple signals for children to walk up toward their own or a neighbor's house. Waiting for the vehicle to pull up and for a man to offer candy or a ride, is waiting too long. They do not have to run in fear. They should simply be told that a vehicle pulling up to them should not be ignored. I am not suggesting that you train your children to go into shock when they see a vehicle approaching. Rather, they can be as curious as they please - from a safe distance.

Even teenagers, especially girls, should be told to carefully watch for parked vehicles containing any occupants. A car which is slowing up near them should be red-flagged as well. In either case, instruct your children to immediately walk up toward a house. Waiting for someone to exit the vehicle is too risky. Also, if they spot a suspicious vehicle, they should quickly look around for anyone else (a possible accomplice) approaching on foot.

• When children are home alone, the door should not be opened for anybody. A man in a police uniform or with a pizza in hand can be explained with one simple phone call. If the knocking continues, a neighbor or police department should be contacted.

Distrust

• Children should be aware that not all "bad persons" are men. You are probably well aware that women have been known to abduct and sexually abuse children. They sometimes team up with men, posing as couples, to fool both children and adults. My question to you is - how aware are your children of this information? Mister Bug-a-boo may not be a "Mister" at all.

• A stranger knowing your child's name or your name can make a big impression on your child. To a child, strangers are people whose names are unknown and who do not know them. Their name being mentioned is a sign that everything is OK. Because in the child's mind, "people who love me and care for me" call me by my name. Children waiting to be picked up from school, at the park or McDonald's, need to understand that anyone, even bad people, can say, "Nicole, your daddy is still working at his office, he wanted me to pick you up and take you home." (It might be a good idea to avoid having your child's name on jackets, shirts, bicycles, etc. for this reason.) In large malls, a young teenager could be suddenly escorted by a member of "store security" without questioning anything. Other shoppers could be fooled as well. Children should also understand that they must never go anywhere with anybody without the presence of others.

• A neighbor, uncle, teacher, etc., could catch them doing something wrong like looking at "dirty pictures" which had been conveniently left out. These pictures, a broken window, stolen candy or any type of "misbehaving" can be used as leverage to coerce a child into a sexually abusive situation. Teach them to avoid allowing an adult to coerce them into sexual activity by blackmailing or threatening them.

Your child must have absolute confidence in your unconditional love. Be sure that he or she understands that nothing can separate them from your love. If they ever do anything wrong, they need to know that your forgiveness is inevitable. Also, inform your children clearly that any sexual abuse

by anybody is wrong and that you will always side with them and attempt to punish the offender. Breaking a window, or running to (or from) a neighbor's house is entirely permissible. At times, saying "NO" to an adult is fine.

• A phone call a child answers can have all kinds of surprises. A friend's daughter was told by someone that she had won a contest through her school which was connected to some boxed cereal. The caller described the gifts and subtly began to verify information on her parents. "Now Heather, let me make sure we have all facts right. Let me see, your dad works away from home, right? Your mother, let's see, it doesn't say whether she works . . . ah, ..wait do they both work or what? Heather was being bated. After over 15 minutes of talking with Mr. Richards, the contest coordinator, Heather's mother asked who was on the phone. Mr. Richards immediately hung up. Heather told her mother that good ol' Mr. Richards was informing her where her prize could be claimed.

• Children also need to know whom they can trust. Generally, they can trust crowds of people with mommies and daddies all over. We once left one of our children behind at a pizza party in a restaurant which had several game rooms. I thought my wife had taken our youngest daughter with her while driving other children home. Since Hannah stayed in another part of the restaurant, several relatives and myself had no idea that she was there. One of my other children neglected to tell me that my wife had told them to tell me that Hannah was to stay with me. As a result, my eight year old was left behind. After arriving at home, I received a call from the restaurant manager. He asked me to hold on. Horror of horrors, I heard my daughter's whimpering voice. A few weeks later, I rented the movie "Home Alone" and laughed my way through it all; all except the part where the mother sat up in her seat and suddenly realized who was missing. It's amazing how easy it is for something like that to happen.

At any rate, my daughter had been told, that if ever separated at a store, mall, restaurant, stadium, etc., to go to the management and tell them that she is lost and for them to call her parents. That makes more sense than to have a child walking around, crying and looking for her parents. A lost child can be spotted by the wrong person. I would rather have a child go to someone who is in authority, than to have someone go to her faking authority.

Instruct your children that if they are ever left behind at school, shopping mall, playground, etc, to never attempt walking home alone. Never, Never. Tell them to dial 911 at a pay phone to call the police. Also have them memorize another relative's or neighbor's phone number for instances when you cannot be reached.

Distract

- Inform your children that it is perfectly fine with you for them to break windows, any windows, provided this is an attempt for them to attract attention and help. Teach them to call out your name in threatening situations even if you are no where in sight. A girl given the keys to the family car should be told what to do with them if attacked. They need to understand that it is perfectly fine to act a little bit out of character if their life depends on it.

The situation may arise (particularly with young children) where an assailant, who is trying to abduct your child, might try to make it seem like the crying/screaming child is simply their own child throwing a fit. Teach your children to convince bystanders that the individual is an impostor, not their parent or guardian. Teach them to say "this person is not my parent, just call my parent at phone # 000-0000.

If your child believes they are being followed, let them know it is perfectly fine for them to let other people know by just saying "That person is following me."

Defend

• Self-defense techniques can be taught at an early age. It is true that body strength and size can limit how effective a child's kicking and punching can be. Nevertheless, learning the mechanics of techniques while young is worth the effort. Poking fingers into the eyes and kicking a man "between the legs" can be learned easily and can work, even for a child.

A couple of years ago, a local newspaper article described how an eighteen year old woman was abducted from a mall parking lot and later repeatedly raped. According to the article, the girl was leaving work with other employees after the store had closed. The parking lot was vacant except for employee vehicles parked on the opposite end of the lot (according to standard retail policy). She said goodbye and started to walk toward her car. Apparently, other employees stood there chatting near the store entrance. As she neared her vehicle, a car pulled up next to her. A man quickly jumped out, ran toward her, grabbed her and began to force her toward his vehicle. All of this happened in front of her friends. Unfortunately, the store employees were unable to run across the parking lot in time to prevent the abduction. All that she needed was a technique or two in order to slow her captor up for five seconds.

Teach your children how to buy time. If anyone ever tries to carry, drag or pull them into a waiting car, behind some bushes or into a vacant building, etc., and if they are completely overpowered and helpless, teach them to fall to the ground or trip the assailant. In seminars, I usually show a self-defense technique which is designed to defend against someone attempting to carry an individual away. This technique can be taught to young children as well. Simply take one or both legs and continuously attempt to wrap the feet between the assailant's legs and then behind each leg. In rape prevention seminars, I have had five year old children trip me up using this technique. It works. It can slow up an attempted abduction and buy precious time.

• If you possibly can, enroll your children in a reputable, professional self-defense program. Through the years, you or others will teach them how to play piano, shoot baskets, bowl, etc. Someone needs to teach them how to protect themselves. Where does this fit in on your priority list of "things to do" concerning your children's activities?

Chapter Nine - TIPS AND TALES

Depart

- Kids are usually quite good at running like the wind when scared to death. I recommend that you do cover one topic with them however. Teach them where to run to. They need to run where other people are. A young child if being stalked or chased may very well perceive home as the only true shelter of safety. Making their way home might be impossible. Houses with lights on, families in cars, stores, gas stations, buildings with people in sight are an immediate refuge. They need to understand that such "good" people can help them as much as dad or mom can. Instruct them how to quickly say that a man is chasing them and trying to kidnap or hurt them. Tell them to ask the people to call the police and to get them out of sight.

- And that's not all. Your children should know that if ever abducted, they need to act as if they wouldn't dare try to escape, but should do so at the first opportunity. They can fool their captors. Attracting the attention of others is critical.

A final note parent(s), trust your intuition when placing your children in the hands of other people. Credentials, reputation and recommendations don't amount to a hill of beans if there is something about that person(s) which bothers and worries you. I made a mistake once in not trusting my own intuition.

Prior to my move to Louisville, Kentucky to attend a seminary, I met the new "Big Brother" of a neighborhood kid my wife and I thought the world of. He, his mother, and an older sister lived in the neighborhood. They were all excited about their new friend. When introduced to this man, I said hello and complimented him on setting aside some of his time to be a "Big Brother. To this day as I am writing this sentence, I cannot put my finger on it, but there was something about this guy that just didn't seem to rest easy with me. I'm usually a little slow to prejudge somebody during a brief introduction. First impressions can be misleading. However, something was not right with this guy. He didn't have a sinister, hardened or criminal look. He had something else which bothered me. He had a guilty look. Spotting that guilty look has helped me avoid some dangers over the years. He said all of the right things, smiled and complimented the boy. But the guilty look was there. That guilty look was hiding some type of motive. I'm not slamming the Big Brothers organization. They're doing a tremendous work with disadvantaged boys. This was just a bad apple in the bunch. I figured that surely the guy was screened and despite my suspicions - OK. Well, he wasn't.

Upon returning from Kentucky, my wife and I visited the boy and his mother. After exchanging hugs and pleasantries with the mother, I asked about her son. "He's upstairs," she said. Something was wrong, bad wrong. He thought the world of us, as we did of him. He knew we were there, yet remained in his room. His mother began to cry. "R-----was abused while you were gone." She didn't have to say another word, I knew who and I had an idea how. She described to my wife and me how the man (I"m using the term loosely) took her son to ball games, movies and on picnics. The problems started when weekends were spent over the man's house. Movies became more and more sexually suggestive. Her son and his other friend who was also invited, did what little boys do, they became curious. Eventually the boys were abused. At that time I was informed that the courts were handling the matter. I make mistakes all the time, but that is one which, God willing, I will never make again, not with my children or others'.

Inform your child that they are not necessarily any safer in the company of other children. Neither are women if accompanied by other women. Yes, there is a certain level of safety in numbers, but that doesn't mean that you or your children should let your guard down. I met a woman in Michigan who was raped while walking home from high school. She was not alone. Another girl from school was with her. While walking past a field, a man jumped out from behind some bushes and grabbed the other girl. As she began to run, he threatened to hurt the other girl if she didn't return. He placed a cloth bag over both of their heads and secured them tightly around their necks. Unable to see, they had no where to run. He continued to threaten to injure one if the other tried to escape. Both were raped.

Tell your children, and remember yourself, that if you are ever in such a predicament, run for your life. He knows that you can probably identify him and he knows that you are going for help. That will be more difficult for him to deal with than two captives. Also, you should instruct your children (particularly if they are small), that if you are ever attacked in front of them, they should immediately run for help. They really cannot help you. This is something your children might not Instinctively want to do. I don't care how shy and withdrawn a young child might be, if he or she sees mommy being hurt, he or she will try to intervene. Help your children to understand by saying, "You can always help mommy by running for help. Bring a big person who can help. OK?"

Several professional organizations, agencies and resources are available to help you in safeguarding your children. Information is also available for children who have been victimized. Refer to the **RESOURCES** list at the end of this book.

DOMESTIC VIOLENCE

As previously mentioned, a serious problem exists whenever the "protectors" of women become their "predators". The problem is further compounded when such predators, functioning as a husband or significant other, reside under the same roof. The end result is commonly referred to as "domestic violence. Since rape is one form of domestic violence, a few words here are in order.

Tragically, a classic pattern usually develops. A man and a woman make arrangements (often marriage) to live together. As time passes, an abusive relationship develops. Verbal and physical assaults become more frequent and severe. Far too often, relatives, friends, neighbors and the police are never informed of the victim's plight due to her embarrassment or fear. If others are told, usually their assistance is simply too little, too late. Be that as it may, here are some things to think about should domestic violence raise its ugly head in your world.

1.Don't accept continuing abuse as your lot in life. Even if your feelings of self-worth are on the low side, allowing an individual to take advantage of your vulnerabilities will only make things worse. Your self-worth is not for the taking by him or anybody else. Your self-worth will increase whenever you do something you think is valuable. Tell him to go prey on somebody else.

2.Nip things in the bud. At the first indication of abusive behavior, whether verbal or physical and regardless of how subtle, express our opposition and contempt. Lash out with righteous indignation. A proper precedent must be set. Abusive behavior will cost him something. It must be clearly understood that mistreatment of you will result in some kind of reprisal.

3.Meet his abusive and aggressive behavior with equal or greater resistance. As his abuse escalates, so should your defense against it. He must understand and believe that in the here and now or any place or time hereafter, you will never under any circumstances accept his violence.

4.Remember that audiences, surprises and a lack of control over their victims, disturb and deter rapists and will most likely work well against anyone committing other forms of domestic violence. He is vulnerable!

5.Inform others of your predicament. Don't limit your call for help to only one individual or group. There is strength in numbers. The more people you have in your corner, the more options you will have available to you.

6.Apply the systematic self-defense system.

Discern early signs of abusive behavior. In fact, before entering into an arrangement to live with another, observe how the individual treats other women.

Distrust repeated "it will never happen again" statements. Such assurances are not guarantees, and are often unreliable.

Distract him by visibly drawing the attention of others to your predicament. Avoid weak and apologetic statements. Focus on your anger, not your fear. Inform him that if he persists, everything will become public record. Call the police. Document everything. Hire a private investigator if now one fully appreciates your situation.

Defend yourself. When push comes to shove, do whatever you can to survive. Remember the time to strike is when opportunity presents itself. Seek appropriate, professional self-defense training. If he is threatening your life, consider purchasing a gun and get some professional training on how to use it.

Depart whenever you can. In the short run, plan an escape if it comes to that. Find refuge with people you can trust. At least initially, keep him guessing where you are. In the longer run, consider departing the relationship altogether.

Note: When it comes to the question of departing a relationship scarred with domestic violence, ask yourself these questions. If things continue as they are, where will it all end? What is the worst thing that can happen if you stay in the abusive relationship? What is the worst thing that can happen if you don't?

SEXUAL HARASSMENT IN THE WORK PLACE

As shown by the Anita Hill ordeal, our country was glued to television sets defining and redefining just exactly what sexual harassment is and is not. The silent crime was finally having light shed upon it. The whole world watched as two individuals did battle with each other - character against character, reputation against reputation and testimony against testimony. I believe that many spectators walked away wondering who was really telling the truth. Many, I'm sure, walked away wondering just what is sexual harassment. It was difficult to pass judgment on who was in the wrong when no one seemed to agree on what "wrong" was.

I attended a seminar entitled "Sexual Harassment in the Work place" presented by Sue Eisenberg and Toni Stafford in November 1991. As part of their presentation, they had participants fill out a questionnaire which had also been given to 1,000 personnel directors and EEO officers. After reading a brief description of an incident, participants were asked to decide whether sexual harassment had taken place and if so, what disciplinary or legal action was warranted. Clearly everyone seemed to have their own definition of sexual harassment.

Betty Harragan offers an interesting description of sexual harassment in her book Games Mother Never Taught You. She refers to sexual harassment as "women's most dangerous occupational hazard" (Harragan, 1977, p. 366). It is Harragan's contention that sexual activity with other employees usually proves detrimental to a woman's current social status as well as future advancement. Of course, what I or others believe is sexual harassment isn't the issue. The issue is what is sexual harassment to you. The pressures which disturb, discriminate and affect you at work because you failed to comply with an employer's or fellow employee's sexual demands is what matters. It is a question of what you are involuntarily subjected to involving unwanted sexual comments, demands and activities while at work. My objective here is not to define what you must define for yourself. Instead, I want to share with you some tips on how to avoid, restrict and terminate the behavior of anyone at work you feel is pressuring you for sexual compliance. Since sexual harassment can often develop into further sexual assault, I am committed to offering you a few tips to defend against it.

Once you discern that an employer or another employee is crossing over the line (your line) verbally or physically, do the following:

1. Immediately begin to document every comment and action which has offended you. Record the date and time; then, report the incident to personnel or upper management if you feel comfortable in doing so. Your company may have an internal grievance procedure.

2. Inform someone at work you can trust or an individual away from work of your predicament. Relate your story to them and show them the documentation.

3. Bring a small tape recorder into work for further documentation. Store all written and taped documentation away from the work place.

4. Witty and coy statements can sometimes nip the problem in the bud.

"John, I thought you were married."

"Mr. Davis, how's your wife? I haven't talked to her recently, but it looks as if I will be."

"I thought I was hired as a typist. If you want a hooker, check out the numbers on bathroom walls."

"Sure you can put that lewd picture in this office, but a court could very well decide that it will eventually carry an eight figure price tag."

"Suppose you and I talk with higher management. I guess you have a different interpretation of my job description."

"You know Frank, I have a strange habit. I keep track of everything. I'm really good at details. No kidding. I can show you what time I arrived for work three weeks ago - Monday. By the way, every word, insinuation and movement of yours concerning your "demand" is there also. Don't force me to buy more paper."

"I hope you clearly understand that what you are doing is unsolicited, unwelcome and illegal. A court of law will determine how expensive."

"I apologize - really - I'm sorry. I didn't know that your mental and sexual development stopped at age eleven. Don't you think that maybe you should be seeing a therapist or something. I mean - I can't help you. Sick people need doctors."

"You're not blushing now, but you will be when I make all of this public."

"Don't direct that kind of behavior toward me."

"It helps to have an attorney in the family. My ex-husband found that out in a very expensive way."

"The next time you say that to me, try to remember every word. You will probably be asked to repeat in court."

Note: Clearly state what activities or behavior is upsetting you. Don't sound apologetic; sound vindictive, antagonistic and upset.

4. Send a letter to your personnel department or upper management clearly stating and documenting your continued problem. Express your appreciation to them for looking into and hopefully resolving the matter. Date and sign the letter with a copy sent to the harasser(s) and to a third party of your choice, perhaps an attorney.

5. File a formal complaint with the Equal Employment Opportunity Commission at 1-800-USA-EEOC or contact a local attorney.

6. Contact the following organizations for additional information and support concerning sexual harassment.

Department of Justice,
Civil Rights Division
320 First Street, N.W.
HOLC Building, Room 832
Washington, D.C. 20530
(202) 724-2240

Women's Bureau,
Department of Labor
200 Constitution Avenue, N.W.
Room S3002
Washington, D.C. 20510
(202) 523-6611

Chapter Nine - TIPS AND TALES

TRAVELING

Following is some information you should keep in mind when traveling.

Automobiles are generally dependable. Now and then, however, they can break down and leave you stranded. As a woman, this can leave you in a precarious position if you are traveling alone. Consider protecting yourself with some precautionary measures.

- Always make a mental note of what road you are on and if possible, what direction you are heading. You can quickly and accurately relay this information via a mobile phone. If you do not have a mobile phone, use a telephone booth only if it is nearby and in a well lighted area. If any cars are slowing up near you or if you spot someone in the area, stay in your vehicle. Again, I recommend that you call the police first and a towing service second.

- A large flashlight can be purchased which has a flashing red or amber light. Placing this in your front or back window can supplement your vehicle's flashers.

- Construct a large, collapsible sign out of posterboard which can be stored under your seat and placed in your back window when needed. Bright, reflective paint and poster-board can be purchased in most art supply stores. Print in large, bold letters the words, **"CALL THE POLICE."** I must admit that I have mixed feelings about such a sign. Although the sign can attract the attention of concerned citizens to call the police, unfortunately it can also inform a low-life cruising in the area that in all probability, a stranded woman is in the vehicle.

- In your glove box, store a pad of paper, road map, pen and pencil. A plastic gun (used to bluff), nail file, pair of scissors or letter opener can be legally carried in your vehicle.

- Your tire jack (handle) can be kept under your car seat as easily as it can in your trunk. It can be used for lug nuts or against someone trying to inflict bodily harm on you.

- In your trunk keep plastic "emergency" flags (available in most hardware stores), a blanket, a gas can, a gallon container of coolant or antifreeze, a small tool box and, if you can afford them, an extra radiator hose, fan belt and roll of duct tape. The spare parts can help you if towed to a gas station which may not have the parts you need or an available mechanic. Someone who is usually trustworthy such as a policeman, or a man accompanied by a family, can usually help you, provided you have these spare parts and tools.

- If you have a CB radio, broadcast your predicament on an emergency channel which is usually monitored by police. Truck drivers have a good reputation when it comes to helping people out. However, I caution you to leave your vehicle only if more than one truck stops.

- The license number and/or description of any vehicle which stops in front of you or passes by and returns should be written down in a notebook and kept in your glove compartment.

If a car has passed by slowly and is looping around to return, and if you are uncomfortable with the situation, write down the word "kidnaped" or "help me." Gerard Whittemore recommends placing several color portraits of yourself in the car (glove box, on the visor, under a floor mat, etc. He recommends that you write on the back of the pictures information which will let police know who you are, where you live, and the time and date when your car broke down. "Include a statement that you will not leave your car unless forced to do so." He recommends writing the license plate number and description of the vehicle and/or assailant(s) on the pictures as well (Whittemore, 1986, p. 115).

- As discussed before, if you are stranded in your car and are approached by someone who orders you to open the door and begins to attempt a forced entry, move away from the door. If you haven't yet grabbed a personal protection device, now is the time. Ask the assailant if it is money that he wants. Offer to throw your purse out the opposite window. If the assailant is attempting to break the glass on one of the doors, quickly move over to the other side of the car. If the assailant gains entry, be prepared to escape out of the opposite door or defend with an object.

- When traveling out of state, remember that your license plate informs local residents that you probably will not be in the area for long. A rapist knows that unless he is identified immediately, he only has to stay out of the public eye for a short period. Once you leave the area, he doesn't have to worry about running into you at the neighborhood shopping center. Simply put, you are more vulnerable when you are an out-of-towner.

- Although valet parking offers you the safety of simply stepping out of your vehicle and into a building, you should only hand the attendant the ignition key. Personal information such as your registration, envelopes, garage door opener and miscellaneous identification should be locked in your glove box (provided the ignition key does not fit it). If that isn't possible, place the information somewhere else where it cannot be easily found.

- When traveling abroad, never let your guard down. I forget which television program covered the story, but an investigation of reported rapes occurring on travel cruises created quite a stir. In fact, one incident involved a woman who was raped in her room while on a cruise ship. Her husband was visiting another area. Conviction of the rapist was apparently impossible since the crime took place in international waters. Attendants, even if criminally suspect and discharged, can supposedly migrate from one cruise line to another. A five star hotel or luxury cruise ship does not necessarily mean that the security is at par with the food or entertainment. Enjoy your traveling but do so with your guard up and a systematic self-defense system.

- If you exit a building, enter your vehicle and notice that it will not start, beware. It could be a mechanical failure or it could be that someone tampered with your vehicle. You should have locked the doors upon entering the vehicle already. Look around for somebody nearby. If

it looks safe, make your way back inside the building. Also, be especially suspicious of anyone suddenly appearing on the scene to offer assistance. It could be legitimate, or an act of entrapment. Slightly open your window and talk to the individual offering assistance, but do not open the door.

- If you are waiting in a car for your companion, be aware of the fact that although they may have only walked into a party store for a gallon of milk, someone could jump in that car, threaten you, start the car and have you on the road in a matter of seconds. The keys should never be left in the ignition and you should make a habit of locking the doors.

Also be aware that when you are sitting in a car, an assailant will most likely approach from what is commonly referred to as the "blind spot". This is the area behind and to the side of where you are sitting.

- Car alarms with a remote panic button which enables an individual to activate the alarm from outside the vehicle is a smart device to invest in. A blaring siren is quite a distraction for a rapist to deal with.

- Kill switches, sometimes called toggle switches, which prevent the car from being started can protect you as well if an assailant is attempting to abduct you in your vehicle. You could simply say that you have no idea why the car will not start. The kill switch should also be used when your companion is inside a store, or gas station, building, etc. This device can usually be installed for $50.00 or less.

- If you get a flat tire in a bad area, drive the car on the flattened tire. The tire rim (wheel) can always be replaced. If your car is overheating, turn the heater on high and drive slowly. Driving with a car that is overheating can do considerable damage and so can someone who finds you alone stranded in your car. Don't be overly concerned about the car. If you feel threatened, drive on. Granted, it is a judgment call, but remember that engines can be rebuilt whereas a sexually abused body and a broken spirit may never heal.

- Beware of the do-it-yourself car wash facilities where you drive your car into a stall, put in the quarters and rinse your car off. While in the stall, someone sneaking up on you can place you in great jeopardy since you are so isolated. I would avoid patronizing them at night. Day light hours would not offer much more safety unless several people were using the facility.

- Servicemen from gas, electric, water, cable TV, etc., should be checked out before they are allowed to enter your home. Politely motion to them through a window that you will be right with them. A one minute phone call to a nearby office can verify the legitimacy of their visit. If bogus, call the police immediately.

- Sometimes while shopping, walking in a park, eating in a restaurant or viewing a movie in a theater, a "pervert" will decide to hassle you. He might decide to whisper sexual filth, stare at you continuously or expose himself in one way or another. In fact, April, my twenty one year old daughter recently experienced what was her first confrontation with a pervert. Both she and Hannah, my 12 year old, entered a drug store to look for birthday cards. Jeff, April's friend from college, had decided to wait in the car. While browsing through cards, April felt someone bumping into her buttocks with their elbow or hand. Each time that she would turn around, the man would turn aside as if looking at the cards. A few minutes later, April was bending down looking at some cards, when this same person walked up close to her with obvious intentions of having April's attention directed toward his groin area. The sight was disturbing to my daughter, and she concluded as well that she had not been bumped by the man's elbow earlier. She immediately stood up to grab Hannah's hand behind her. She walked toward the checkout counter to inform the cashier that a man had been fondling her and in a sense exposing himself. Unfortunately, she had barely finished her sentence, when she noticed that the man had already slipped by and was hurrying out the door.

I don't take such incidents lightly. If a man will do extreme things publicly, it is probably only a matter of time before he will increase his thrills by abducting a woman and increase his humiliation tactics. I called the Troy police department to report the incident and then I had some additional advice for my daughter. In such situations:

- Immediately, draw attention to your predicament by exposing the pervert. You might feel more fear than anger, but don't let him know that. Even if you have to act a little out of character, act mad or get mad. To borrow from Mr. Spock, create a "force field" of anger.

- Get loud and if necessary get crude. Scream loudly or yell statements that will get his attention and the attention of others.

"Back off pervert!"

"Don't direct that kind of behavior toward me."

"Someone help me, this guy is a pervert!"

"Brian come here, this creep is bothering me."

"Someone call the police, this guy is touching me."

- Try to see what vehicle he walks toward and if possible get the license number. Try to observe as much as possible about the assailant. This information will assist the police to apprehend him.

- If you are unable to confront him verbally, then knock something off a counter and create a disturbance.

- Under no circumstances, do you leave the store by yourself. Call the police and wait for them to arrive. If, for whatever reasons, you choose to not make a police report, have a store employee accompany you and look for the pervert in the parking lot. Make sure that you are not being followed after you leave the parking lot.

- When walking around corners of buildings, cars, vans, bushes, etc., make a wide turn just in case someone is lurking there.

HOME SECURITY

Alarm Systems

Whether you live in a house, condominium, apartment or are temporarily residing in a college dormitory or motel, the dwelling should be safe and secure. Living with others does help, but others are not always there with you. Following are some helpful tips on securing the premises where you are currently residing.

Security (Alarm) Systems

In 1990, I helped to design and develop a course in home security systems which was eventually taught to UAW - Chrysler and Ford employees. Having worked for a company which sold, installed and serviced commercial and residential alarm systems, and having helped in the installation of my own system, I was familiar with the technology and equipment. The course was designed to equip students with the technical knowledge and skills to design and install their own security (alarm) system.

Those experiences gave me a good understanding of the wide range of home security equipment which is available today. As I researched home security systems, I became totally convinced that a security system is probably the best way to protect yourself and your property. Although I think decorative security (storm) doors, wood and metal doors secured with dead bolt locks and bars on windows can offer protection, they can only visibly and physically deter someone from entering into your dwelling. They cannot protect you as you are walking through your back door.

If someone attacks you while you are entering, you are on your own. Also, most of the doors are opened with keys and anything key locked or activated can be tampered with. Ask any policeman about that statement. With an alarm system, you can both discern (in this case detect) and distract an unwanted intruder.

I recommend installing a passive infrared (PIR) motion detector inside your residence. This can be turned on when no one is home. If someone decides to break into your home and wait for your return, they're in for a big surprise. The motion detector will be activated by their presence and will cause the alarm to go off. With this device, a woman can be confident that no one is waiting inside for her return. No matter how an intruder enters the building, they can be detected by the system once inside. Alarm system salesman will call this interior protection.

Perimeter protection refers to exterior doors and windows. Alarm system companies have several types of detection switches to choose from. I always favored magnetic switches. Some others were too sensitive to strong winds, loud noises, lightning, etc. I recommend securing doors and windows also since this serves with exterior lighting as your first wall of defense. Incidentally, the new exterior lights which have PIR sensors are a great idea. When someone walks near the sensor, your exterior light comes on.

Having the system monitored by a central station is a good idea if you can afford it. You can't always depend on neighbors to respond by coming to your assistance or calling the police when they hear your alarm sounding.

Perhaps the most important devices to have installed are panic buttons. I recommend one on each level of your home including one in the master bedroom. The benefit of having panic buttons is that even if your alarm system is not turned on, and someone walks through a screened door, all that you have to do is press the button and the alarm will be activated. If the system is monitored, the central station will know that the panic or duress button has been pressed suggesting a life-threatening situation. There are hand-held panic buttons, resembling small garage door openers, which can be carried in your purse, pocket, etc. They can activate the system from a distance, while you are inside or outside of your residence.

If you live in an apartment or are renting a home where the walls cannot be tampered with, wireless systems are available with interior sirens which are quite loud. Again, I highly recommend alarm systems not just to protect your belongings, but to protect you. Contact at least three companies and get a price from each on identical systems. Ask each company for some references and make a decision from there.

Doors and Windows

Putting an extra lock on an outside screen/storm door is a good idea since most of the factory installed locks can be easily jimmied. Latches and eye hooks can be purchased at any hardware store. Placing an extra lock may not necessarily make forcing open the door impossible but it sure can create more noise and frustration for the individual trying to sneak through it. Dead bolt locks and sturdy doors are important and well worth the money you might have to spend to buy them. The more glass that you have on a main door, the less strength and protection will be available.

If you have double hung windows, you might consider opening the window about a foot and then drilling a hole into the side of the window frame just above the window. Place a metal peg in the hole. This will prevent someone from quietly cutting the screen (especially on newer vinyl types) and simply pushing up the window. To get in, the intruder will be forced to break some glass and make some noise if the window will only open enough for fresh air to pass through. Also in case of fire, a quick exit would still be possible by simply removing the screw or peg.

Leave more than one interior light on when you leave your home and alternate which lights you leave on. Timing devices which automatically turn lights on are available at most hardware stores. Remember, keep the criminal mind guessing. Try not to be too predictable. If you see someone parked near your home when you leave, act as if you are waving goodbye to somebody inside. This will keep whoever is in the car guessing. Of course, it may get your neighbors wondering about you. Oh well.

If you live in an apartment or condominium which has a cubby hole or small opening into the attic, then you should secure that opening so that someone cannot simply lift up the covering and slip down into your living quarters. Often, the attic is one large area which can be accessed by any apartment or condominium within the building. In other words, anyone entering the attic can then easily have access to another apartment

While living in a townhouse, my brother-in-law discovered that a small opening in the ceiling of a closet (cubby hole)

gained access to the attic which covered all of the other dwellings. Essentially, anyone entering the attic could then easily gain access to other townhouses the same way. In fact, someone had been laying above their bedroom and had chiseled a small hole from which to eavesdrop. Again, you can see why I highly recommend an alarm system. A motion detector could detect anyone in your apartment when you are not there.

Personal Protection Devices

Sounding Devices

I gave my daughter a compact, hand-held sounding device which emits a 104-decibel sound when activated. The device which is approximately 2" x 3" has a cord which if pulled disconnects the cord from the device and activates an ear piercing sound. While away at college, she carried it in her purse with the cord hanging out while in public. In her dormitory room, she placed the device near her bed at night.

Sprays

Mace, pepper and tear gas sprays have been around for a while. With a direct hit, they can help you defend against a rapist. However, there are a few things that you should know about such items. Heavily intoxicated or drugged assailants have a higher resistance to such sprays. Rapists can see that you have the device and can charge you with his head down to avoid a direct hit. Also, these items can be used against you. I think that they can help, especially CS tear gas, but don't think for a minute that you can put a self-defense system in a can. Incorporate such devices into yourself-defense system.

Last year I saw an interview with the inventor of a spray described as a criminal identifier. I contacted the man and met him in Detroit to discuss the product. A former Toronto police officer, he grew tired of trying to place suspects at the scene of a crime and came up with a device which can remedy the problem. The product is called DyeWitness, a pressurized can of green spray which can be sprayed at an attacker from a distance of six or seven feet. A spray which leaves a stain on the skin is nothing new. Banks have used such solutions for years to mark money. He simply personalized the idea. Granted, the spray can identify a criminal by marking him with a green stain which is next to impossible to remove, but I like the product for another reason. Unlike the other sprays, this is one self-defense devise which cannot really be used against you. If the spray touches you, then the assailant cannot touch you without being stained as well. Also, as in gang rape, a woman surrounded by five men would have a difficult time defending herself even with a baseball bat in hand. Yet with this spray, she

could quickly stain the attackers, and, like the window breaking technique, show that she resisted and hopefully convince the attackers that their dyed skin will be called into question by somebody somewhere down the line. Anyone attempting rape could later claim that they were no where near the victim. Fortunately his green skin would suggest otherwise.

I think it has tremendous psychological value when it comes to rape prevention. The product is available in the United States. I wish they had injected red pepper in the spray. There are some drawbacks, however. The canisters are pressurized and can explode if left in a car during hot weather. The company recommends changing canisters after six months.

Guns

I recommend that you have a gun to protect yourself with. I have read most of the arguments for and against owning guns, and nothing has swayed me away from my position. I believe that your constitutional right to bear arms is quite clear. Your right to use lethal force in self-defense is protected by law as well. For an excellent presentation of the pros and cons concerning owning guns for self-defense, read Paxton Quigley's Armed And Female. For opposing views, read Pete Shield's Guns Don't Die - People Do and The Second Amendment Foundation's The Gun Culture And Its Enemies which is edited by William R. Tonso.

When confronted by a rapist, what does having a gun in your hand accomplish?

1. A gun is universally accepted as a respectable means of defense. It usually gains the immediate respect of an assailant.

2. A gun will enable you to protect yourself from a distance without physically risking making contact.

3. A gun can distract a rapist.

4. A gun offers both psychological and physical defense against an adversary. Either the sight or the explosive impact of a bullet will deter a rapist.

5. A gun offers you an immediate means of lethal force if nothing else can stop a rapist's advance.

6. A gun can be used to protect you in a gang rape situation. When confronted by several assailants, a gun and you make a majority.

7. A gun in your possession can significantly increase your self-confidence in life threatening situations.

8. A gun can back your verbal statements.

9. A gun can be carried with you (legally) provided you can justify

the need. One example of such is a concealed weapons permit for business purposes.

10. A gun is not difficult to use if you receive proper instructions.

By the way, especially if you are a woman who lives alone, I recommend that you keep a gun loaded. I'm sure that some readers will question that statement because children may be placed at risk. Paxton Quigley comments on this predicament. "Having a gun for security and keeping it safe from others are mutually antagonistic. The safer the gun is, the less ready it is for emergency use; the more ready a gun is to be fired, the more opportunity there is for mishaps." (Quigley, 1989, p. 117). You have to weigh the risks.

You keep medicines in your home to protect children, and yet you risk them tampering with them. What do you do? You recognize the value of their presence, but you store them in a safe area and warn your children of their inherent dangers. Having sick children without medication is much like having a rapist in your house with no protection. If you contact the National Safety Council or the Consumer Product Safety Commission, you will find that guns are not nearly the "threat" that you might think compared to other causes. Compared to death by motor-vehicle accidents, drowning, fires/burns, poisoning, etc., death by firearms is low on the list.

Chapter Nine - TIPS AND TALES

Significantly more people are injured each year through activities such as bicycling, football, gymnastics, etc. than handling firearms.

I have received firearms training and can tell you from first hand experience, that loading an empty gun with limited time can be difficult. During training, I noticed that although the stopwatch was the only "enemy," it was a nerve rattling experience. I am sure that hearing an intruder break into your house and attempting to load a gun at 2:00 in the morning can be a hair raising experience. Keep the gun in your bedroom where it can be easily reached in an emergency, but where children and thieves cannot easily discover it. Your children should be informed that the gun is real, can kill and is not to be touched. A trip to a local gun range can erase any curiosity which children may have. A locking device on the trigger is not a bad idea if your children are prone to get into things. The key must be easily accessible, near the gun, yet not readily available to children. Following are a few pointers for children:

- Remind them of the old adage that "Empty guns kill."

- Never point a gun at anything or anybody.

- Do not show neighborhood friends, relatives, etc. where the "family" gun is kept.

- Never put your finger on the trigger. Never, never, never!

- The only time that a gun is to be fired is under your supervision and only at a gun range.

- If ever curious or "wondering" about the gun, ask and you will be shown. There is no mystery. Guns can kill, whether by accident or by design.

Guns fit well into a systematic self-defense system since they can distract an assailant and can be used most effectively to defend against him. Criminals universally agree that a gun in the hand of a targeted victim is not a pleasant site. Government studies back my recommendation for you to protect yourself with a gun. In 1985, the U.S. Department of Justice published an interesting study titled The Armed Criminal in America. Researchers asked convicted criminals a series of behavioral questions. Following are some results of that study.

- 40% decided not to commit a crime whenever they suspected that the victim was armed.

- 34% reported that a targeted victim who was armed either shot at them, scared them off, wounded or captured them.

- 57% agreed with the statement that "Most criminals are more worried about meeting an armed victim than they are about running into the police."

Government statistics show that 71% of the women who took "self-protective" measures were not victims of a completed rape. I wonder how many of those women had a gun. A gun in your hand can give you a tremendous psychological edge over someone contemplating raping you. A gun barrel facing a man attempting to rape you will instantly remind him that a confrontation will not last long. He knows that one squeeze of a trigger can place a hot piece of lead in his body in a fraction of a second.

What type of gun is best suited for women is another important consideration. My wife has a Colt .38 special. I chose this revolver for the following reasons:

- The gun has ample stopping power without the forceful recoil and over penetration found with .357 and .44 Magnum revolvers. A revolver is simple to operate. You simply pull the trigger and the gun fires.

- The size of the handle and weight of the gun is ideally suited for women.

- The gun is relatively inexpensive.

Another excellent gun for personal protection is the 9mm automatic. This gun has good stopping power and can be fired as rapidly as you can repeatedly pull the trigger. Police departments are increasingly changing over from the ever popular .357 Magnum to the 9mm since it can hold from 14 to 18 bullets (depending on which model is chosen) and can be fired rapidly. The rise in the usage of automatic weapons by criminals has forced law enforcement officers to reconsider the effectiveness of the .357 revolver. As long as you can comfortably operate the slide on the top of a 9mm, this is a fine choice for personal protection. Visit a local gun shop and ask someone to show you how to operate the slide. If the movement is too difficult, then perhaps you should avoid using a 9mm.

Most experts agree that when it comes to stopping power, a shotgun is hard to beat. Massad Ayoob, a well-known authority on gun protection and the use of lethal force, recommends a handgun as the primary choice of defense and a shotgun as the ultimate backup weapon. "The shotgun is the most devastating combat weapon available to the civilian." (Ayoob, 1980, p. 100). Police departments all over this country agree with Ayoob. Look in the front seat of any police car, and guess what you will see? A shotgun in your hands will increase the heart-rate of a rapist quicker than any medication known to mankind. Even the distinctive sound of a shotgun being racked is intimidating. Although most police departments use a 12 gauge shotgun, a 16 or 20 gauge has plenty of stopping power and can be handled by most women. If you point this gun in the general direction of your assailant, he knows that his chances of being hit are very high. Ayoob recommends using buckshot (small pellets) as ammunition in a shotgun for home defense. When that trigger is pulled, an assailant has several pellets coming his way at a high velocity. The impact is severe and so is the damage.

Whether you choose a .38 Special revolver, 9mm automatic or a shotgun, you need to understand something about a gun, or any other weapon. To use a weapon effectively, you must have the will and the knowledge of how to use it. A local gun range might let you practice shooting each weapon to decide which is best suited for you. Some gun ranges offer courses on gun usage and safety. You will be amazed how proper training can quickly familiarize you with a weapon and increase your ability to use it. Police departments can also offer advice on local shooting organizations and can inform you on the legal requirements for purchasing and registering a gun.

Anti-gun groups repeatedly proclaim that guns kill while gun advocates remind their adversaries that guns also protect and save lives. The debate rages on. However, when it comes to protecting yourself from rape, an important consideration is what a rapist thinks. He knows that a targeted victim who has a gun in hand will not be easy prey.

Another important consideration is the opinion of a court of law. If you defend yourself by shooting an assailant, what guidelines will a court use in justifying or condemning your use of lethal force?

Massad Ayoob, in his book IN THE GRAVEST EXTREME, clearly defines justifiable use of deadly force (Ayoob, 1980, pp. 5-24). According to Ayoob, there must be danger of death or grave bodily harm which is both immediate and entirely unavoidable. To legally justify using lethal force, three conditions must be present.

1. The assailant must have the **ability** to perform the attack. He or she must have the ability to kill or cause severe injury or have what Ayoob calls "disparity of force" which in my mind implies an unfair advantage.

2. The assailant must have a legitimate **opportunity** to commit the crime. He or she must be "in a position where he is obviously and immediately capable of carrying out a threat."

3. The assailant's behavior must cause the victim, as a reasonable and prudent person, to believe that his or her life or limb is in **jeopardy**. "Altogether, the best rule is to resort to

deadly force when life and limb are in jeopardy. American laws universally condone homicide only when undertaken to escape imminent and unavoidable danger of death or grave bodily harm." In other words, a paralyzed man confined to a wheelchair screaming threatening words to you from the opposite side of a parking lot would not meet the ability, opportunity and jeopardy conditions. On the other hand, if you are in your home and confronted by an intruder who is lunging at you with an apparent motive to do great, bodily harm and you have no immediate means of escape, the weapon in your hand can be used to defend yourself even if it means killing the attacker. Movies give you the impression that you have to shout "Freeze," "Stop," "Don't move," and after doing so, even armed assailants will simply oblige by dropping their weapon. According to Ayoob, ". . . in real life, the criminal does not freeze at the unexpected challenge. If he does not pull the trigger automatically as he faces you, it will be the first response that occurs to his hair-trigger nervous system when he sees you" (Ayoob, 1980, p. 59). If you reasonably and prudently believe that someone is immediately and unavoidably attempting to severely injure you and/or rape you, and if there is no means of escaping, aim the gun and pull the trigger. Personally, if the assailant does not have a gun, then I suggest you clearly state, or shout, "Stop or I'll shoot!" If he doesn't stop, then shoot. If he stops, have him lie face down on the floor; then, call the police (if a phone is near). If no phone is near, order him to leave; then, call the police. If you are forced to shoot an attacker, aim for the center of the torso. Continue firing if the attacker continues to advance. Once the attacker is stopped, he no longer has the ability and opportunity. Your life is no longer in jeopardy. Escape if you are able. If not, go to another area and call the police but be sure that you remain prepared to shoot the attacker should he revive and continue the attack. My opinion is that when the police arrive, I would make the following statements.

A. I felt that my life was being threatened.

B. I shot in self-defense.

C. Any other statements will be made with my attorney present.

I'm not attempting to draw a picture here of law enforcement officers as the "bad guys." They're on your side all the way. I have the highest respect for them. My suggestion is that you simply be very careful of what statements you make before you have an opportunity to settle down. If you feel uncomfortable answering certain questions, DON'T. Attorneys will later hold you accountable for statements made immediately following the ordeal. I don't push it too far, but the old saying, "I'd rather be tried by twelve than carried out by six" has some truth in it when attempting to protect your life.

Besides your local police department and gun shops, the following organizations are available to help you in learning more about guns for personal protection.

National Rifle Association of America
1600 Rhode Island Avenue, N.W.
Washington, D.C. 20036

Handgun Control, Inc.
1400 K Street, N.W.
Suite 500
Washington, D.C. 20005

The Firearms Coalition
P.O. Box 6537
Silver Spring, MD 20906

Second Amendment Foundation
James Madison Building
12500 N.E. Tenth Place
Bellevue, Washington 98005

Defensive Training, Inc.
P. O. Box 665
Niwot, Colorado 80544
(303) 530-7106

International Shootists, Inc.
P. O. Box 5254
Mission Hills, California 91345
(818) 891-1723

U.S. Practical Shooting Association
P. O. Box 811
Sedro Woolley, Washington 98284

One final thought on guns. When I was a little guy, my Grandmother used to be a caretaker for an apartment building in Highland Park, Michigan. I used to spend the night there whenever my parents needed a break and my Grandmother needed a challenge. She carried an automatic pistol with her which was nothing more than a replica of a real gun. According to her, it fooled a few people when fooling people was her only way out of a situation. My wife has a plastic replica of a 9mm Beretta pistol, complete with a removable clip, we keep under the car seat. It's a toy my son grew tired of a few years ago. It shoots nothing but air, but that's for us to know and others to worry about. If my Grandmother were alive, she would be smiling.

Just after I concluded a rape prevention seminar at a nearby community college, a woman came to the front of the room. She stood there patiently waiting for a chance to talk with me. I noticed that she seemed extremely distressed. After talking to a few people, she reached for my hand, shook it and said, "Thanks for what you did here tonight. You were right in what you said. I only wish that I had heard this ten years ago." As she began to cry, I began to think about how ten years had not healed all of her pain and hurt. The thought also occurred to me that the 90 minute seminar had contained few words of comfort for victims. I am not sure that I would have had any words of comfort to give. But watching her cry, convinced me that I had to try. I asked her if she wanted to talk about it. She replied that she did, but not then. She said she would appreciate my calling her. I called her the following night.

During the phone conversation, she briefly described how her attack took place. As a sixteen year old, she had double dated with a cousin. The two guys had broken English and seemed to have a lower opinion of women than what she was used to. While sitting in the back seat, she noticed that her cousin and friend seemed to want some time alone. She and her date decided to go for a walk. During that walk, she was raped. She never told anybody, not even her hus-band until recent flashbacks of the event began to affect her. I believe she mentioned that she was seeing a counselor. She began to cry and I began to look for words. I told her that I was sorry about what had happened to her, really sorry. I didn't know if I had the right things to say. As a Christian preaching in jails or nursing homes, I often found that my oratorical, theological and homiletical skills were marginal at best. Nevertheless, I never had a problem accepting my shortcomings. I always figured that God would give me the wisdom and vocabulary to get the job done since due to His providence, that is where He put me. Following is a recollection of some thoughts I shared with her:

"You mentioned that you were sixteen years old when you were attacked. Although I'm sure that it seems like yesterday, that's a long time ago. In many ways, you are not the person that you were then. Your appearance has probably changed (I had to be careful with that statement). You think differently. I'm sure that you act differently. In fact, life around you has changed quite a bit too. In the scheme of things, what happened to you then, happened to a different person. You can never be that sixteen year old again. The past can never be changed. Only in your mind, can you go back to that time and you must do so on the wings of your memories. What-

Chapter Ten - WORDS OF COMFORT

ever you do on this earth cannot change that sixteen year old you once were. Similarly that sixteen year old cannot affect you now unless like many elderly I have visited in nursing homes, you begin to live your present life in the past. I can understand that in a nursing home. Precious memories hold less pain and confusion than the present.

However, for you it's different. We're talking about one specific time in which life didn't meet you half way. Sometimes it just doesn't. Don't let that one event from the past define life for you in the present or in the future. Don't do it. You were a rape victim. You are not a rape victim now. Something happened to you which just should not have happened; but it did. And you're not alone. Everybody has had something happen in their life which hurt them in some way - something which simply should not have happened. It was not fair, and it was not right. It just happened. That is a great mystery in life. Some people have faired better than you and some have not. But I'll tell you this, my hat goes off to people who have overcome life's disappointments. Sometimes life will throw you banana peels, it doesn't mean you have to collect them. About the lowlife who raped you, don't worry, he will get his. What goes around - comes around. As Charles Dickens would say, he is nothing more than a "shadow from the past." Whenever I think of someone from the past whom I get upset thinking

about, I remember what my pastor once said, "The man you're angry with won't let you sleep."

Think about it. When you dwell on this guy and what he did, anger probably builds up in you. Who is it hurting, you or him? The memory of that night is like a dog. The more you feed it, the more it will grow. I did ask her if she was a Christian like myself. She said that she was. Then I reminded her what Corrie Ten Boon, a Christian woman who lost family members and endured the atrocities of the Nazi concentration camps once said. "There is no pit so deep, that God is not deeper still." Whenever God's grace is needed, it will be there. I usually mention one or more of the following Bible verses.

"For I am persuaded, that neither death, nor life, nor angels, nor principalities, nor powers, nor things present, nor things to come, Nor height, nor depth, nor any other creature, shall be able to separate us from the love of God, which is in Christ Jesus our Lord." Romans 8:38,39

"Blessed be God, even the Father of our Lord Jesus Christ, the Father of mercies, and the God of all comfort; Who comforteth us in all our tribulation, that we may be able to comfort them which are in any trouble, by the comfort wherewith we ourselves are comforted of God." II Corinthians 1:3,4

Chapter Ten - WORDS OF COMFORT

"I can do all things through Christ which strengtheneth me." Philippians 4:13

"But my God shall supply all your need according to his riches in glory by Christ Jesus." Philippians 4:19

I have always been told and have always believed that all of God's stories have happy endings. I did share with her as I am you, that my faith is strengthened by attending church. This is one place where a rape victim may choose to seek comfort.

If attending a church is out of the question, most major cities have several rape crisis centers/clinics and shelters for sexually abused women. The staff in such organizations is generally well acquainted with the atrocities of rape. They have experience in accompanying rape victims to hospital emergency rooms, local police departments and to the victim's residence. Any phone directory in your area will probably have a listing of such organizations. Also, most hospitals and police departments have staff with specific training to cater to the needs of rape victims.

Even if you are reluctant to press charges against the assailant, information shared with police investigators can possibly assist them in identifying him as a suspect for other sexual attacks, and apprehending him.

If you decide to report a rape, remember that everything in, on or about you can be used as evidence. According to Joy Eyman, "The right medical evidence, presented in a dramatic and coherent manner, can be enough to convict a rapist. This does not mean simply the presence of sperm or seminal fluid. The precise documentation of scratches and bruises, and other signs of a struggle, can be as persuasive in the minds of jurors as laboratory tests" (Eyman, p. 29).

As illustrated by Madelyn's incident, victims often want to "shower" away the refuse and cleanse themselves. Eyman further states "The fact that evidential material is being taken does not mean that the victim must prosecute. Evidential material is so fragile that it must be taken immediately or it may be lost forever." If you later decide to prosecute, at least you have something to take to court. Remember, rapists sometimes choose to attack the same victim again. If not, there will be another victim waiting in the wings. There is a considerable amount of "relief" in knowing that you "got even" legally.

A final note: I felt compelled to write this chapter. Although it does not concern rape prevention as such, I believe that rape has touched the lives of too many women. Perhaps you have not needed to hear any words of comfort and, hopefully, will not need them in the future. My guess is that most readers know somebody who has, or will.

Chapter 11 - Final Thoughts

Only you can prevent forest fires.

- Smokey Bear

Do you remember the bear dressed up in a forest ranger's uniform saying that? That statement reminds me of what I have been suggesting throughout this book. For the most part, you are most responsible for your safety. Only you can prevent yourself from being raped. Others can help from time to time, but in a 24 hour day, the largest load of responsibility when it comes to safeguarding yourself against rape, lies on your shoulders. Beyond the information which has been previously presented, there are several things you can do socially and politically to protect yourself and others from being raped. Someone needs to stop testing the water and jump in with both feet. Men will support you, but I think you and other women collectively need to take the lead on this one.

Women in this country are besieged with the fear of being raped, some more than others, but all to some degree. On the other hand, except for those incarcerated in prisons, men in general have not spent much time thinking or worrying about being raped. Their concerns are usually limited to women they know and care about. Their motivation to jump on a rape prevention bandwagon is different from most women's. That is something which they need to

come to grips with and change. But again, it will be women who must get things rolling. If you don't, who will?

Since becoming involved with helping women in the area of rape prevention, I have lectured to many women of all ages. I have written this book. I will be producing a video series on rape prevention and someday I plan to open self-defense centers which focus on practical self-defense and rape prevention. The training objective will be to equip participants with the psychological, physical and verbal skills required for effective self-defense. I am also interested in forming a national organization or advisory board to address personal protection from crime. I am doing just about all that my time and finances allow. I recommend that you and other women do the same.

There are some large groups in this country that are committed to expanding and protecting women's rights. Ladies, let's not forget a woman's right not to be raped.

In addition to applying the principles and techniques recommended in this book, you should consider the following recommendations.

- Track the sentencing records of judges in your state.

- Evaluate the decisions of parole boards and the therapeutic success rate of psychologists working for

Chapter 11 - Final Thoughts

each state's Department of Corrections. Investigate and verify how state and federal funds are allocated to address the rehabilitation or lengthened incarceration of sexual offenders.

Consider, the plight in my home state of Michigan. As I am writing this book, Michigan prisons are currently housing about 4,500 sexual offenders including rapists and child molesters. According to an article in the Detroit News/Free Press, August 1, 1992, Dr. John Rushbrook, Chief Psychologist for the Michigan Department of Corrections, performed a computer analysis of Michigan's rehabilitation and therapy problem. He discovered that 2,800 convicted sex offenders are eligible for parole or will be within two years. Rushbrook also discovered that prison psychologists are treating only about one thousand. This is even more alarming when you consider the high rate of recidivism involving sexual offenses

According to the article, John Prelesnik, warden at Mid-Michigan Temporary Correctional Facility, "I've got 400 sex offenders here right now and we only have 33 in therapy." The article also offers a short profile on Terry Alexander, a convicted rapist. Terry was released from prison in 1988 after receiving four years of "rehabilitation." Terry had completed his third prison term for rape.

Whenever he was released, he raped again. Eight years of prison had not changed Terry. According to the Detroit News/Free Press, Terry, after starting therapy, was quoted as saying, "I know I am ready. I have full control over my past repugnant condition." No he didn't. Seven months after his prison release, Terry kidnaped a 15-year old girl in Muskegon, Michigan, raped her and stabbed her six times in the chest. The girl was later found with both lungs collapsed and in shock. Someone treating Terry Alexander blew it. The parole board blew it. A young girl suffered the consequences.

Another case in point involves Leslie Williams (referred to earlier) who received 14 months of therapy while incarcerated for a rape conviction. After being released, Leslie raped and killed four teenage girls. Someone blew it again. This time four girls suffered the consequences.

In this country, prison systems are not rehabilitating sex offenders, they are warehousing them. To make matters worse, no one is held accountable. You and other women need to check that out. Who is responsible for this travesty? To a certain degree, you and I are, if we allow it to continue.

And that's not all. The eye-opening Detroit News/Free Press article also quoted Elizabeth Alexander, who is an attorney with the American Civil Liberties Union. She has been involved with a prison project in Washington, D.C. According to Alexander, "The studies on recidivism show the two factors that correlate most highly with whether someone in prison is going to go back to crime are whether that person maintains family ties and whether he can get a job. If you were deliberately trying to design a prison system most likely to protect the public, you would be critically concerned about rehabilitation." Elizabeth Alexander is exactly right. Having counseled several incarcerated men, I have often heard that financial and employment problems heavily influenced the initial decision to turn to crime. After prison release, financial and employment problems resurface. Unemployed due to an "ex-con" status and an absence of marketable skills, men soon find adjusting to society most difficult. I truly believe that training incarcerated men and instilling in them responsibility will do much in modifying their behavior patterns.

I also agree with Dr. Rushbrook's statement. "Before we (Department of Corrections) even consider a sex offender fit for release, I'd like to see an external control system. A spouse, a parole agent, a parent, an employer - someone has to know that he is a sex offender."

Please don't misunderstand the above statements. I disagree with the sentences which convicted rapists currently serve. I do not justify the crimes of any rapist. A convicted rapist forfeits his right to live within our society until he serves the sentence "we the people" have declared should be served. I don't care what their childhood, social status or bad breaks in life consisted of. Raping a woman or child to release socially induced anger, or to "do unto others" what was once done unto you, or lashing back at a society which has not "treated you right" does not, will not, and can never justify committing rape.

Charles Colson in an article which he wrote in Christianity Today (September 1989), lashes out at psychologists and educators who sympathetically explain the uncontrollable impulses of "depraved" rapists. His statement addresses the issue directly, honestly and in my opinion - accurately. "Violent tendencies are not an illness. Criminal behavior is not a symptom of a disease. We cannot explain away awful acts through sociological factors or odd chromosomes or poverty or germs or drugs. While these can surely be factors in criminal behavior, the root cause of crime has not changed since Cain. It is sin." I agree with Mr. Colson.

However, the laws of the land rule, not my opinion. If by law, a convicted rapist must be freed after serving a specific sentence, then prison systems must use that time to effectively rehabilitate prisoners. This measure will protect women and children as well as the convicted rapist. The entire process must take place under the watchful eye of an "external control system" - not a few, but all of us.

I received a letter from Charles Colson on behalf of the Prison Fellowship. Mr. Colson sheds some interesting light on our failing criminal justice system. I found the following statistics supportive of my position.

- The United States has more people in prison than any other nation. For every 100,000 citizens, 500 are incarcerated somewhere.

- The prison population is growing at a rate ten times faster than the growth of the general population.

- The cost of constructing new prison facilities is approximately $80,000 per cell. The annual cost to incarcerate an inmate is $18,000 per year. You are paying for a failing system.

- Eighty percent of all crimes are committed by former prisoners.

"The only real solution is changed hearts."
- Charles Colson

3. Inform the schools, colleges and citizens within a community that a sex offender has been released and due to parole mandates, is living in the area. The June 1, 1987 issue of Time magazine examines the reaction a California town which protested the California State Department of Correction's decision to "place" a convicted rapist in their area. The rapist had served eight years of a 14-year, four-month sentence for hacking off the forearms of a 15-year old hitchhiker. The state claimed that he had paid his debt to society whereas community residents chanted "He must go!" The California Supreme Court turned down the county's appeal to override the corrections department "right" to place the convicted rapist in their town. (Time, p. 31). The courts may mandate a parolee to live in your area, but your freedom of speech allows you the right to inform each other of his presence.

4. Question candidates running for public office concerning their views on the rape issue in this country.

5. Psychiatric institutions who treat sexual offenders should be evaluated and monitored to determine whether "cured" patients are released, only to commit the same atrocities.

6. If you don't have a neighborhood watch, then you should consider forming one. The group's activities should include:

- A monthly or quarterly meeting
- An emergency meeting should the need arise
- Telling neighborhood children which homes are safe refuge
- Reminding neighbors to monitor any unfamiliar vehicle which seems to be circling or cruising through the area

7. Encourage local schools to develop an awareness program for students which caters to students K-12. As the children age, the information should become more comprehensive.

8. Make sure that your children and other neighborhood children clearly understand that they can seek emergency refuge at designated homes nearby (time permitting) and any home if the need arises.

9. When discerning potential danger, always remember to keep a keen eye for detail such as the license number, model and color of a vehicle and the size, color, clothing and distinguishing features of an individual. Remember, that men and women have been known to team up to abduct and rape women and children.

10. Organize an association or advisory committee which can focus on . . .

- Performing lobbying activities
- Monitoring press releases, court rulings and sentencing,

and pertinent television and radio programs

11. Contact shopping malls and national chain stores and encourage them to do what I have been recommending for some time. Have them implement a parking lot monitoring system.

I do not believe, and neither should you, that a security vehicle or an occasional unmarked car cruising around the parking lot offers sufficient protection. Even when periodically supported by a local police department, a large parking lot can be a nightmare when it comes to surveillance.

As a former reserve police officer in Livonia, Michigan, I accompanied another officer in a squad car while patrolling a large mall. He remarked that even though marked and unmarked police cars cruised the area with the mall security patrol, cars were stolen all the time. Shoplifting, breaking and entering of vehicles, purse snatchings and assaults were still a major problem. Holiday shopping made things worse. Women could be so much safer and abduction and rape statistics would plummet if surveillance towers or buildings were positioned in different areas. I see little, yellow Photo-Mat cubicles all over the country. What is wrong with installing small, attractive surveillance stations on top of a building or in the center of a parking lot? The windows could be mirrored or tinted. Surveillance cameras and spot lights could be used to immediately film and draw attention to where a crime is being committed. The cost would not be significant. Besides I think that mall owners and retailers have a moral, ethical and perhaps legal obligation to protect their paying customers and employees. And while I'm on the subject, retailers who direct their employees to park in a designated area away from the store entrance should also provide protection for those employees when they leave the building. Security patrols usually are hard to find once businesses close but what about a seventeen year old female employee who after cashing out her till is leaving twenty minutes later. Hmmm. Those surveillance centers could make a considerable impact in the area of rape prevention. If located on a roof or attached to a building, these surveillance centers would keep any individual contemplating assaulting, abducting or raping a woman guessing. He wouldn't know whether he was being watched or filmed would he? He can spot patrol cars and security patrols. In fact, here in Michigan several shopping malls use security vehicles which have yellow flashers turned on while patrolling an area. Criminals can often spot unmarked cars as well. They learn to spot "the law." But they can't see through mirrored or tinted glass, can they? Remember what I said about keeping an assailant guessing. He will be.

Minimally, large malls or stores should install surveillance cameras on the exterior of buildings or on parking lot poles. They would help, but the surveillance cubicles would pose a bigger threat since an assailant's biggest fear is the presence of others. Individuals contemplating a crime would not even be able to determine whether the cubicles were empty or not. What an excellent public relations effort this could be for a major retailer. It would send a strong "WE REALLY DO CARE ABOUT YOU" message.

12. Contact your phone companies and ask that phone cords be lengthened on public phones to allow for you to comfortably turn around while talking. Also, a small mirror built into the top of a phone would offer some protection. The longer cords would allow more feasibility if you had to use the phone piece as a weapon.

13. Automatic teller machines (ATM) should have mirrors built in at head level so that while using the machine, you can spot someone walking up from behind.

Businesses offering ATM's should also consider modifying the machine so that they include the following:

• Panic or alarm button which either sounds an audible alarm and activates a flasher and/or sends a duress signal to a police department. Perhaps to avoid false alarms, an individual would have to gain access to the system before the panic or alarm button could be activated.

- A surveillance camera which is activated as someone approaches the ATM.

To borrow a few words from Johnnie Carson on his last show, "We'll I guess it all comes down to this." It is time to wrap things up. I would have savored the luxury of having more hours in the day to research additional material for this book. I find myself thinking of information which should have been inserted in earlier chapters. I have come to fully understand what a friend of mine meant when he said that "the perfect book is the one that is never finished." I have had my turn at bat, and I am thankful for that.

I sincerely hope in reference to my writing objectives listed in the introduction, that -

1. You are safer from being raped in this country than you were prior to reading this book.

2. You are more psychologically and physically prepared to defend yourself.

3. You have read this book with an open mind.

4. You have been properly motivated and prepared to look at the current rape epidemic squarely in the eye.

5. You have developed, and will further develop, a systematic self-defense system which includes principles and techniques which are designed to distract, confuse and deter a rapist.

Remember the questions and answers, predictable routines and their shortcomings, Madelyn's and my sister's states of panic, the statistics, a rapist's ever-present vulnerabilities and how to exploit them, the systematic self-defense system (5 D's), the stretching exercises and techniques, the words of comfort, the tips and tales and the final thoughts. Do your homework. Set aside a few hours each week to practice and further develop your systematic self-defense. Teach your children.

Strengthen your belief and conviction that no one has the right to rape you. Expand your rape prevention options and your bag of tricks so that if ever confronted by a rapist, you will effectively outwit, outsmart and outmaneuver him throughout the ordeal. Shatter his fantasy by breaking a window. Refuse to take part in his little plot by throwing away the car keys. If you don't like the rules of his twisted game, then change them. Play by your rules.

Chapter 11 - Final Thoughts

Always distance yourself and buy time. Control your breathing (remember the quarter). Remember the creep who talks funny in St. Louis and the hard boiled eggs. Remember, that you are your own best defense.

Dear reader, I hope that you never have to ask a rapist "What part of NO don't you understand?" I hope that you will so thoroughly, and systematically defend against him that every part of NO will be understood.

I wish you well!

RESOURCES

National Organization for
Victim Assistance
1757 Park Road, N.W.
Washington, D.C. 20010
(202) 232-6682

National Association for
Crime Victims Rights, Inc.
P.O. Box 16161
Portland, Oregon 97216-0161
(503)252-9012

National Crime Prevention Council
733 15th Street N.W.
Washington, D.C. 20005
(202)393-7141
6 East Monroe 1502
Chicago, IL 60603
(312) 332-5540

U.S. Department of Health and
Human Services
National Center for the Prevention
and Control of Rape (NCPCR)
5600 Fishers Lane
Rockville, MD 20857

National Institute on Rape
P.O. Box 2325
Berkeley, CA 94708

PGH Action Against Rape, Inc.
P.O. Box 10433
Pittsburgh, PA 15234

National Center for Missing and
Exploited Children
1835 K Street, N.W., Suite 700
Washington, D.C. 20006
1-800-843-5678

Home Run: A National Search
for Missing Children
P.O. Box 590473
San Francisco, CA 94159
(619) 292-5683

U.S. Department of Health and
Human Services
P.O. Box 1182
Washington, D.C. 20013

National Committee for the
Prevention of Child Abuse
332 South Michigan Avenue
Suite 1250
Chicago, Illinois 60475
(312) 663-3520

Society's League Against
Molestation
P.O. Box 833
Beltsville, Maryland 20623
(301) 952-0063

Society for Young Victims
5 Washington Street
Manchester, Massachusetts 01944
(617) 526-1080

Lost Child Network
P.O. Box 6442
Shawnee Mission, Kansas 66206
1-800-843-5678

Families Aware of
Childhood Traumas
P.O. Box 99
Carle Place, New York 11514
(516) 338-4945
(516) 334-0971

Parents Against Molesters
P.O. Box 12591
Norfolk, Virginia 23502
(804) 465-1582

BIBLIOGRAPHY

Amir, M. 1971. Patterns in Forcible Rape. Chicago: University of Chicago Press.

Ayoob, M. 1980. In the Gravest Extreme. Concord: Massad F. and Dorothy Ayoob Publishing.

Brownmiller, S. 1975. Against Our Will: Men, Women and Rape. New York: Simon and Schuster.

Bureau of Justice Statistics. 1991. Female Victims of Violent Crime. Washington D.C.: Department of Justice.

Colson, C. "You Can't Cure the Wilding Sickness," Christianity Today, Sept. 1989.

Eyman, J. 1980. How to Convict a Rapist. Briarcliff Manor, New York: Stein and Day.

Estrich, S. 1987. Real Rape. Cambridge, Mass.: Harvard University Press.

Griffin, S. 1971. Rape: The All-American Crime.

Holland, L. 1989. New Reasons to Report Rape. Goodhousekeeping Magazine, August, 1989.

Koss, M. 1987. The Rape Victim: Clinical and Community Approaches to Treatment. Lexington, Mass.: The Stephen Greene Press.

MacKellar, J. 1975. Rape: The Bait and the Trap. New York: Crown Publishers.

Quigley, P. 1989. Armed and Female. New York: E.P. Dutton.

Shields, P. 1981. Guns Don't Die - People Do. New York: Arbor House.

Slaby, A. 1989. After-Shock: Surviving the Delayed Effects of Truam, Crisis and Loss. New York: Villard Books.

Sliwa, L. 1986. Attitude: Commonsense Defense for Women. New York: Crown Publishers, Inc.

Storaska, F. 1975. How to Say No to a Rapist - And Survive. New York: Random House.

Tonso, W. 1990. The Gun Culture and its Enemies. Bellevue, Washington: Merril Press.

United States Department of Justice, F.B.I. 1991. Crime in the United States: Uniform Crime Report. Washington, D.C. U.S. Government Printing Office.

Vanninni, V. and Pogliani, G. T. 1980. The Color Atlas of Human Anatomy. New York: Beckman House.

Warshaw, R. 1988. I Never Called It Rape. New York: Harper & Row.

Whittemore, G. 1986. Street Wisdom for Women: A Handbook for Urban Survival. Boston: Quinlan Press.

Zal. H. 1990. Panic Disorder - The Great Pretender. New York: Plenum Press.